Mastering SAP Enterprise Portal 6.0 Appl

Renald Wittwer

Contents

1 Introduction

Application development and portal programming in the SAP Enterprise Portal 6.0 environment requires, first and foremost, that you are able to differentiate between the technologies available and decide which one to use.

This SAP PRESS Essentials book introduces you to the possibilities available for developing portal applications. After reading this book and executing all the examples contained in it, you will know how to use the Web Dynpro technology for application development, how to load required data from your SAP system, and how you can integrate the application into your portal. You will learn how to use business server pages (BSPs) and integrate them into the portal. Further, you will be able to apply a role-dependent behavior in order to make an application available to different user groups.

The book introduces the benefits and drawbacks of Web Dynpro and BSPs to you so that you can use this information to make future platform decisions without the user noticing the technology you used to implement your application.

Many of the techniques presented in this book are also contained in various tutorials in the SAP Help Portal (*http://help.sap.com*). However, in this book they are discussed in a single coherent context. The development of a complex target scenario enables us to describe the individual issues as in a "real-life project."

1.1 Approach

This book is divided into four parts.

In the employee portal (**Chapter 2**), we'll begin with a Web Dynpro application for displaying sales orders. The application should look like the one shown in Figure 1.1. In that application, you can use the customer number and sales organization as filter criteria for selecting all sales orders of a specific period. By clicking on a sales or-

der item listed in the display, you can then view the detail data of the entire order. The customer number originates in the R/3 system and identifies the customer. The sales organization is responsible for the sales and distribution of materials and services.

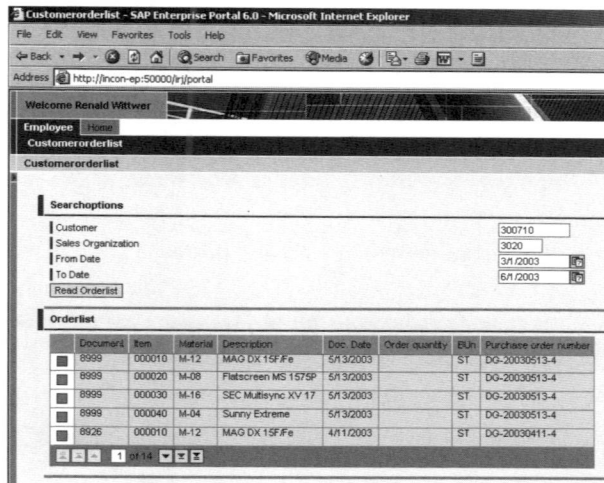

Figure 1.1 Sales Orders List

We'll use the same application in the customer portal (**Chapter 3**) with the restriction that the customer number and the sales organization can't be entered, because a customer can select only his own sales orders. We'll store the customer number and the sales organization with the portal user and determine them at runtime.

In the partner portal (**Chapter 4**) we'll develop a BSP application in which we'll demonstrate the use of HTMLB, among other things. That way, we'll create a list of employees in which you can make selections by last name and first name and generate a results list that includes phone numbers and email addresses. For this purpose we'll use the existing employee data from the SAP system (see Figure 1.2)

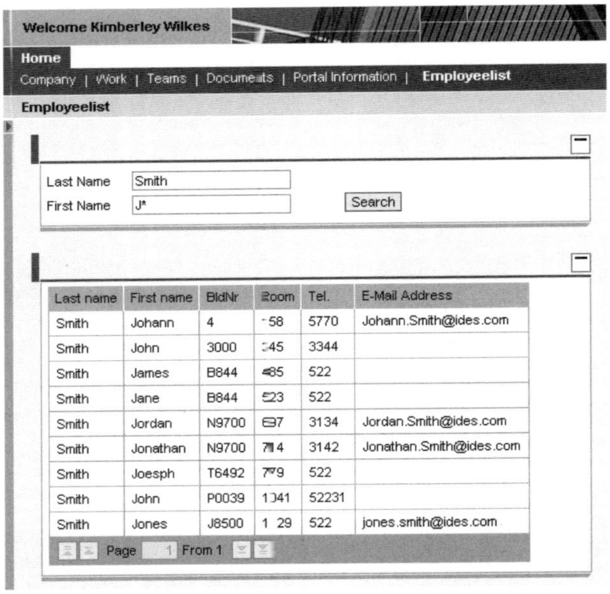

Figure 1.2 Employee List

The tips and tricks in **Chapter 5** refer to more general subjects. In that chapter, you'll find useful information on the configuration of your portal and the installation of the Sneak Preview that's available from SAP Developer Network (*http://sdn.sap.com*). Moreover, you'll get information on typical troubleshooting issues during the development phase and on successfully debugging a Web Dynpro application.

1.2   Acknowledgments

A book like this can't be written without the help of others. First of all I'd like to thank bpc AG, particularly Tobias Zierau. Without the support of best practice consulting AG (bpc), which allowed me to use its technical infrastructure, I wouldn't have been able to complete the book.

Furthermore, I'd like to say thanks to the many SAP Developer Network users whose contributions often inspired me to come up with new ideas and led me in the right direction.

My sincere thanks go to Nicole Scharnhorst for supporting my efforts when revising the text.

My final thanks go to Stefan Proksch at Galileo Press for his support and trust during the production of this book.

> **Note** Some of the code listings in this book were optimized for print in a two-column layout. To indicate where a line break is necessary because of the layout and so as not to be included in the actual code, we have inserted the "¬" character. Please pay particular attention to potential blanks that may appear before this character; indentations in subsequent lines of code are only made for a better readability.

2 Employee Portal

We'll begin our sample project with a very simple application: A portal user will be enabled to display the sales orders of a customer, including all details. We'll reduce the information to be displayed to the minimum of required details in order to preserve clarity and to increase the user acceptance of the application (see Figure 2.1). For this purpose, we'll create a Web Dynpro project, describe all required components, import the read-function modules from an R/3 system, and design the user interface of the application. Finally, we'll launch our new application from the portal.

We'll use the application in the customer portal (see Chapter 3) to provide the same functionality to our customers. Naturally, we have to build in a restriction so that the customers can only see their own sales orders.

Web Dynpro or Business Server Pages?

Before we start developing, however, we must answer an important question: Which technology do we want to use in the development process? In the SAP Web Application Server environment, that question basically focuses on the decision between *Web Dynpro* or *Business Server Pages* (BSP).

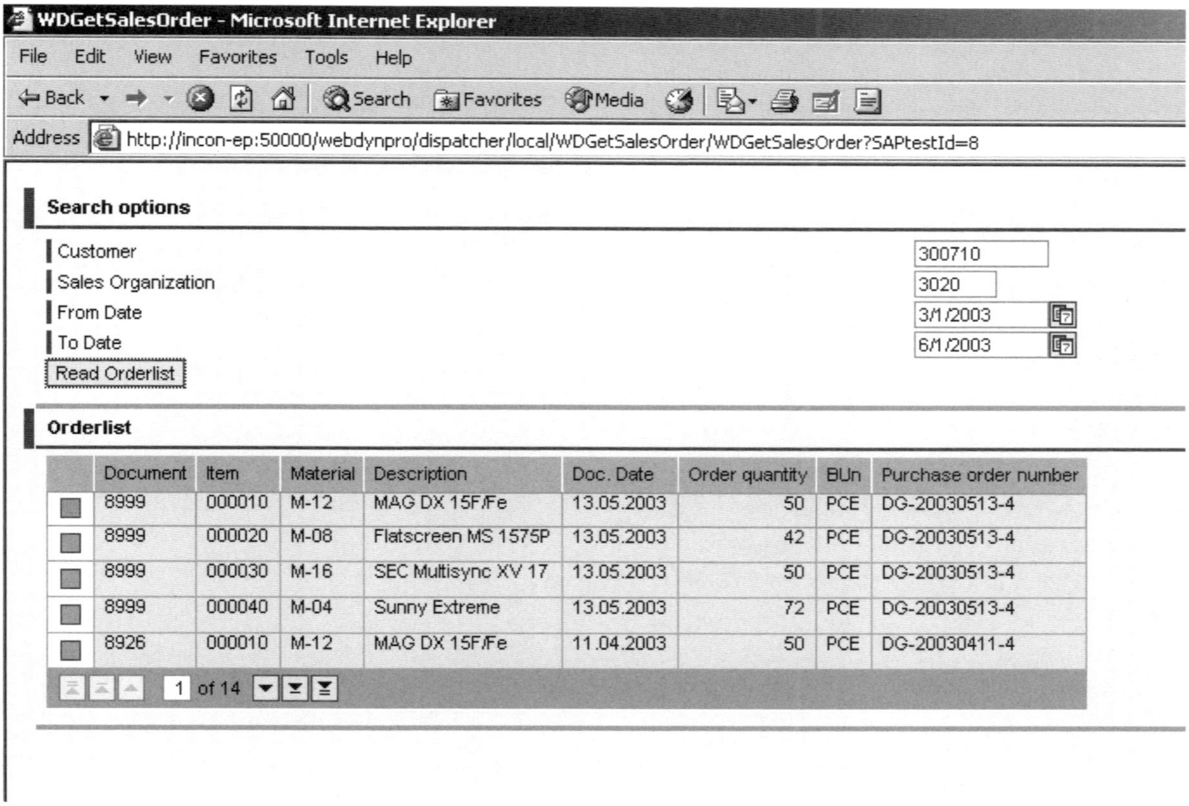

Figure 2.1 Sales Order List

We'll develop our application as Web Dynpro because this enables a closer coupling between the portal and the application than BSPs can provide. Moreover, we'll have better options for checking the role of a logged-on user. Another reason to opt for the Web Dynpro technology is the fact that Web Dynpro can be regarded as a strategic goal of SAP, which means that future developments will be based on this technology. This ensures strong protection of your investments in proprietary development.

Nonetheless, this book focuses on a *comparison* between BSPs and Web Dynpro, and it's not about taking sides. Apart from the aspects discussed in this book, it is important to always consider the environment in which portal applications are developed: Which technology matches the existing resources? Are there any requirements to be met during the development?

At present, Web Dynpro means developing in Java, whereas BSPs represent ABAP development. Note, however, that—as of the next SAP NetWeaver release—Web Dynpro will also be available as an ABAP variant.

Function Modules Used/System Status

For the following procedures, we used an IDES system, Release 4.7. The function modules from the sales and distribution module (SD) however, have been available since Release 3.1H.

2.1   Displaying Sales Orders

The application consists of the following three components:

▶ Home page with search options
▶ Sales order list
▶ Order details

The search options and the sales order list will be located on one page, while the order details will be placed on a second page. Figure 2.2 illustrates the screen flow of the application.

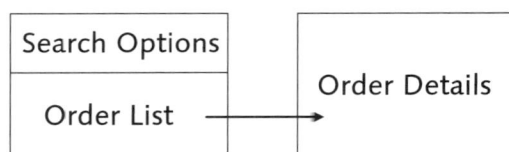

Figure 2.2   Screen Flow of the Application

On the home page, the user should be able to enter the *search options* according to which the sales orders can be identified. We want to make life as easy as possible for him or her and define intelligent pre-settings. The *sales order list* is the result of the search with search options from which you can navigate to the order details.

The *order details* should be made as reusable as possible, and various options are conceivable especially for the display of order details. It should also be possible for other applications to access the order details page. This can for instance be achieved by including the order number as a URL parameter.

Creating a Web Dynpro Project

You can create your first Web Dynpro project by performing the following steps.

1. Start SAP NetWeaver Developer Studio by clicking on the corresponding icon on your desktop or via **Start · Programs · SAP NetWeaver Developer Studio**. Select **File · New · Project** from the menu.

2. The dialog box **Select – Select a wizard** opens (see Figure 2.3), from which you can select an appropriate wizard. Select **Web Dynpro** in the left-hand pane and **Web Dynpro Project** on the right, and confirm your selection by clicking on the **Next** button.

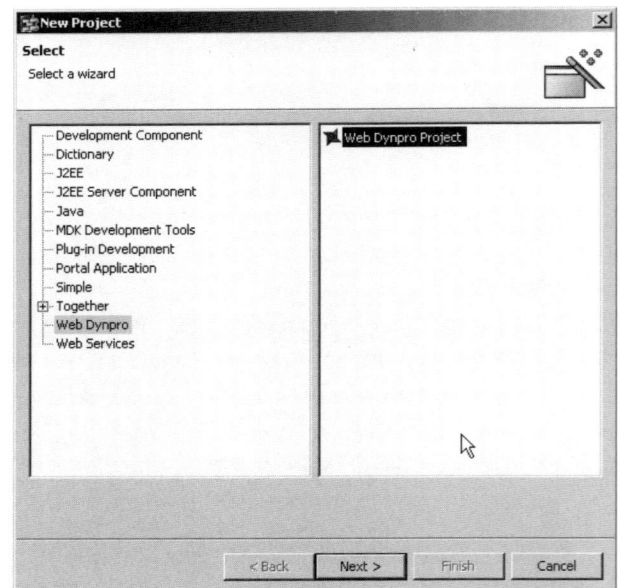

Figure 2.3   Creating a New Project

3. The wizard navigates to the selection screen **Project properties – Create a new Web Dynpro project resource**. Enter the name of our Web Dynpro project in the **Project name** field, in this case that's "WDGetSalesOrder" (see Figure 2.4). The first two letters "WD" stand for Web Dynpro; they are followed by the predicate "Get" because we'll only have read access to the sales orders. Then follows the term "SalesOrder," which describes the object to be read. If the naming conventions in your company differ from those we use here, you should stick to your company's policy. Click on the **Finish** button to confirm your entries.

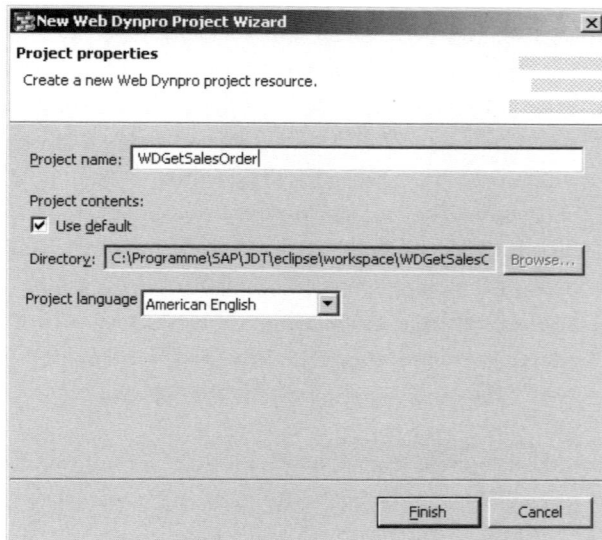

Figure 2.4 Project Properties

A new Web Dynpro project is created automatically, and the wizard then navigates to the Web Dynpro perspective (**Web Dynpro Explorer**). This provides a view tailored for the needs and requirements of a Web Dynpro developer (see Figure 2.5). Here you have access to all relevant development functions, objects, and wizards. In the following sections we'll describe the options provided in the Web Dynpro perspective in more detail.

Creating a Web Dynpro Component

The project we have just created already contains all relevant project structures. However, what is still missing are the elements in which we can store the functions, layout, navigation, and event handlers. For this reason, we

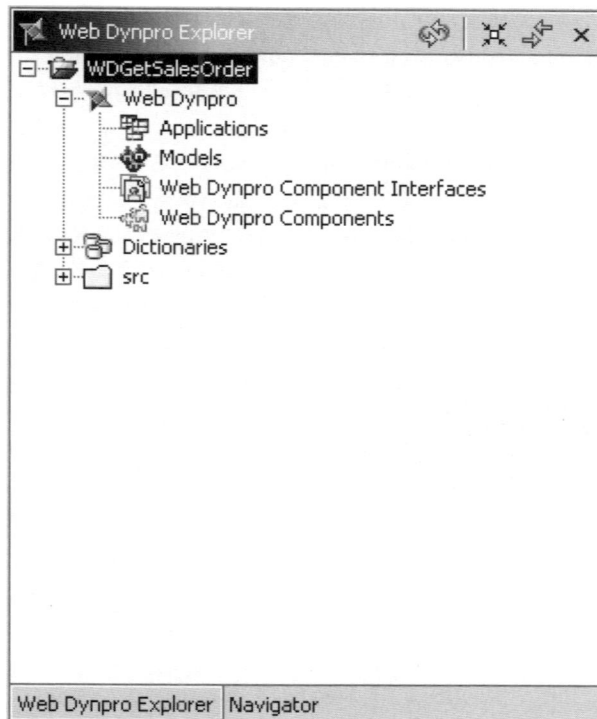

Figure 2.5 Web Dynpro Explorer

need a Web Dynpro component. Web Dynpro components are reusable within the application and encapsulate entire business processes. Web Dynpro components can also be used in other Web Dynpro applications, provided a Web Dynpro development component (DC) has been created.

1. In SAP NetWeaver Developer Studio, go to the Web Dynpro perspective, if you aren't there already. You can do this either via the menu path **Window · Open Perspective · Other · Web Dynpro** or by selecting **Open Perspective** from the navigation bar on the left of the screen.

2. Open the nodes **WDGetSalesOrder · Web Dynpro** of our new Web Dynpro project.

3. Open the context menu of the **Web Dynpro Components** node by right-clicking and select the menu item **Create Web Dynpro Components**.

4. Enter "GetSalesOrderComp" as the **Component Name** and "com.sap.getsalesorder" as the **Component Package**. The name of the component is similar to the name of our application with the addition of the suffix "Comp," which stands for component. Because the package name should be unique even

across company boundaries, it is common practice to use a company's URL in reverse order (here: *www. sap.com*). The package name is supposed to be unique within this namespace.

5. You can copy all other settings. Click on **Finish**.

The `GetSalesOrderComp` component was successfully created for our project. The component wizard has automatically created various objects that are now contained in the newly created component (see Figure 2.6).

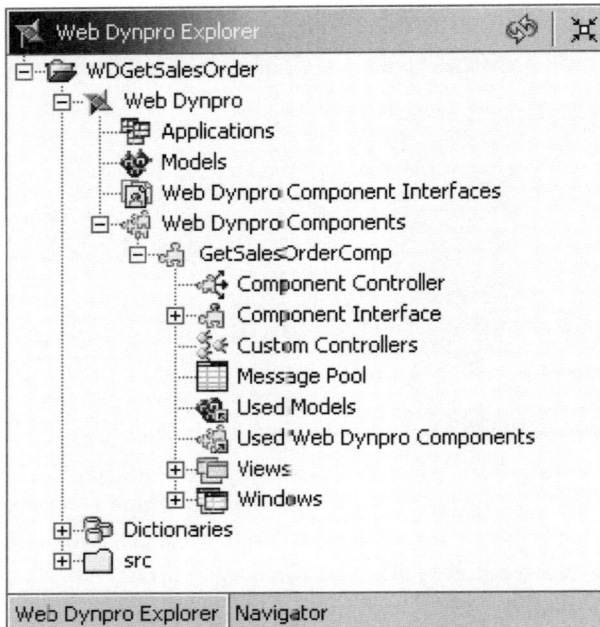

Figure 2.6 Web Dynpro Project Including Component

MVC Concept

Web Dynpro was developed on the basis of the *Model View Controller Concept* (MVC). The *model* encapsulates a specific part of a business process, such as the creation of a new document, and thus functions as an interface to the business process layer. The *view* is the layer in which the user interaction takes place. This layer should not contain any functionality that goes beyond the graphical presentation of user information. The *controller* acts as a link between the model and the view. Most of the implementations in a Web Dynpro application should be contained in controllers.

Creating a Model

The model defines the source and structure of the data that is read. We'll use an RFC (*Remote Function Call*) module to connect our Web Dynpro application to the model. In the first step, the RFC module provides a list of sales orders from one customer. For this purpose we'll use the function module BAPI_SALESORDER_GETLIST.

1. In SAP NetWeaver Developer Studio, go to the Web Dynpro Explorer, if you aren't there yet.
2. Open the nodes **WDGetSalesOrder · Web Dynpro** of our new Web Dynpro project.
3. Right-click on the **Models** node and select **Create Model**.
4. In the selection screen **Select – Choose the model type you want to create**, select **Import Adaptive RFC Model** and click on the **Next** button.
5. The model is defined in the selection screen that opens next. Enter the values shown in Figure 2.7, and click **Next**.
6. In the next step, you must enter the connection data for your R/3 system. This connection data is used only for the model creation; the RFC call connection will be defined at a later stage. Depending on your system environment, select either **Single Server** or **Load Balancing,** and enter the logon information. Click **Next**.
7. If the connection could be established, the system now displays the **Select RFC modules** dialog. Enter "BAPI_SALESORDER*" as a value in the **Function Name** field, and click on **Search**. The system then displays all RFC-enabled function modules that match the search request.
8. Select the function module **BAPI_SALESORDER_ GETLIST** (see Figure 2.8), and click on the **Next** button.
9. The definition of the function module is imported and the result is displayed in the import log. Click on **Finish**. If the system doesn't display any error message, the model has been imported successfully.

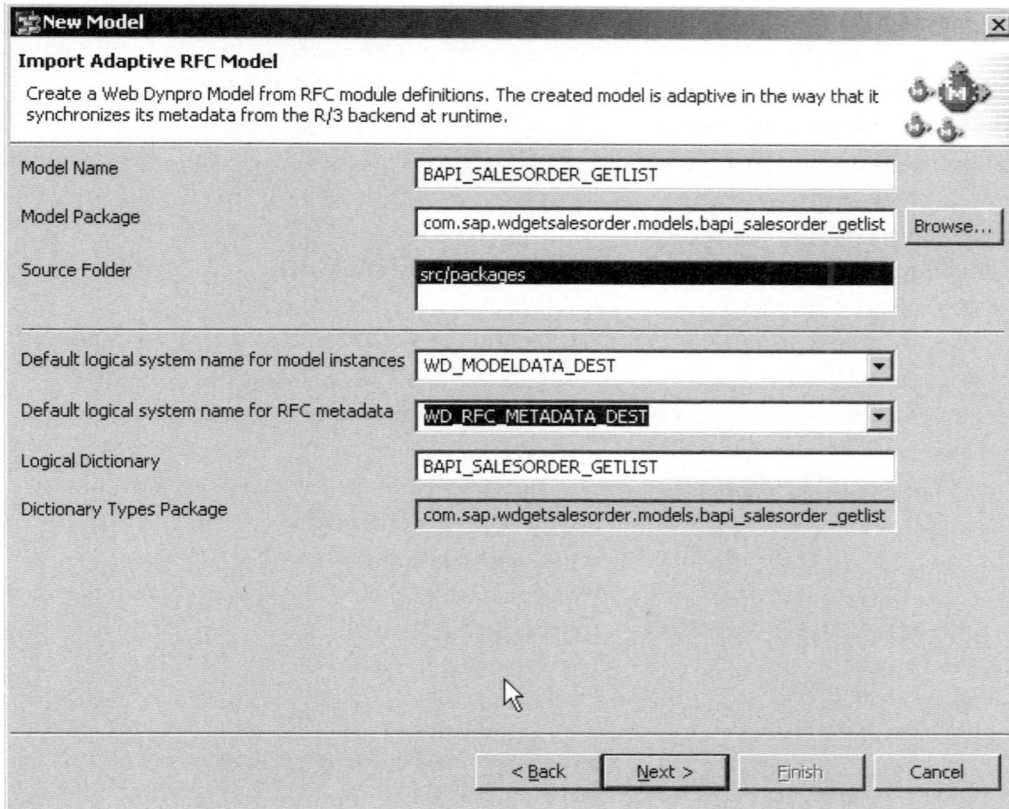

Figure 2.7 Model Definition

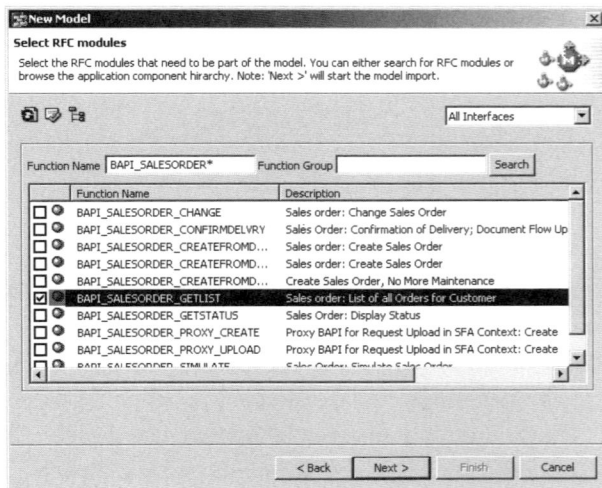

Figure 2.8 Selecting a Function Module

1. Open the nodes **WDGetSalesOrder · Web Dynpro · Web Dynpro Components · GetSalesOrderComp**.

2. Right-click on **Used Models** and select **Add** from the context menu.

3. Select the newly created model **BAPI_SALESORDER_ GETLIST** in the selection screen **Selection Needed** and click **OK**.

4. The node **BAPI_SALESORDER_GETLIST** is now displayed as a child of the **Used Models** node. This means the controller now knows the model and can see it.

Creating a Custom Controller

The central location for implementing a component is the component controller. However, if you want to encapsulate specific functions, you can create custom controllers, although you shouldn't overdo this option.

We now want to summarize the access to the model in a separate custom controller. For this reason, we'll cre-

Connecting Models and Components

To be able to access the model from a controller we must make it known to the component.

ate a custom controller in the following steps after which we'll connect the model to it.

1. Open the nodes **WDGetSalesOrder · Web Dynpro · Web Dynpro Components · GetSalesOrderComp**.

2. Click on the **Custom Controllers** node in the context menu and select **Create Custom Controller**.

3. In the **Controller properties** dialog, enter the value "GetSalesOrderCust" into the **Name** field and leave all other values unchanged. Click on **Finish**.

Connecting Custom Controller and Model

After creating the custom controller (GetSales-OrderCust), we must map the relevant input and output structures of the model. This way we can directly access the structures of the model from the custom controller.

1. To do that, open the nodes **WDGetSalesOrder · Web Dynpro · Web Dynpro Components · GetSales-OrderComp · Custom Controllers**.

2. Right-click on the **GetSalesOrderCust** node and select **Edit**. Alternatively, you can double-click on the **GetSalesOrderCust** node. Depending on the SAP NetWeaver Developer Studio settings, the system then displays the detail view of the controller on the right-hand side of the screen.

3. In the lower part of the detail view, you should see various tabs. Select the **Context** tab, if it hasn't been selected yet.

4. Open the context menu of the **Context** node and then select **New · Model Node**.

5. Select a name for the new **Model Node** in the dialog that opens next. Enter "EAPI_SALESORDER_GETLIST_INPUT" and click on **Finish**.

We have now created a new node in the context (see Figure 2.9) that we are going to connect to the model in the next step.

1. Click on the context menu of the new model node **BAPI_SALESORDER_GETLIST_INPUT** and select **Edit Model Binding**. If this option is deactivated, you haven't connected the model correctly to the controller. In that case you should verify whether you have performed the previous steps correctly.

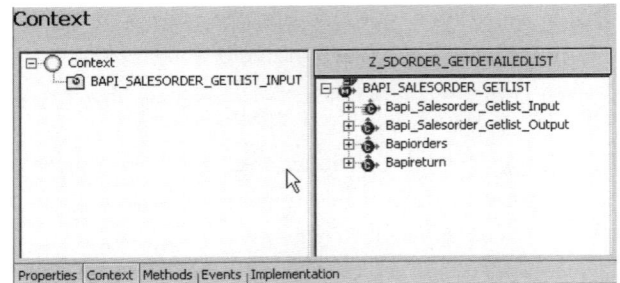

Figure 2.9 Context after Creating the Model Node

2. Click on the **BAPI_SALESORDER_GETLIST_INPUT** node, and then click **Next**.

3. Select the following entries (see Figure 2.10):
   - ▶ **Output · Return**
   - ▶ **Output · SalesOrders**
   - ▶ **Customer_Number**
   - ▶ **Document_Date**
   - ▶ **Document_Date_To**
   - ▶ **Sales_Organization**

4. Click on **Finish**.

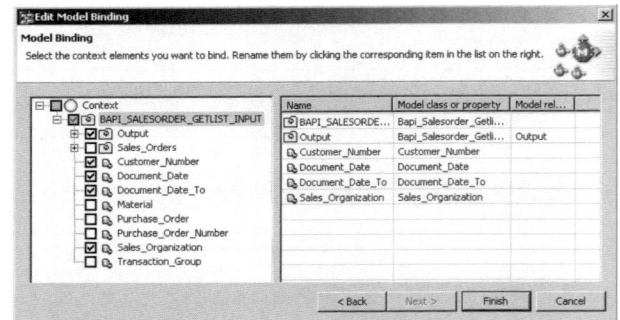

Figure 2.10 Model Binding

Defining the Custom Controller Method

In our custom controller GetSalesOrderCust we need a method that can be used to trigger the BAPI execution. For this purpose, we'll create a separate method, using the following steps.

1. The custom controller **GetSalesOrderCust** should still be open from the previous step. Click on the **Methods** tab.

2. Click **New** to create a new method.

3. You can select the method type in the dialog that opens. Click on **Method** and then **Next**.

4. The name of the new method is "executeBAPI_SALE-SORDER_GETLIST". Keep the **Void** value for the **Return Type**. Click on **Finish**.

Connecting Custom Controller and View

To use the newly created custom controller in the view, we must first connect it to the view.

1. Open the nodes **WDGetSalesOrder · Web Dynpro · Web Dynpro Components · GetSalesOrderComp · Views**.

2. Right-click on the **GetSalesOrderCompView** view and select **Edit**.

3. A dialog opens in the right-hand part of the screen in which you can edit the view. The lower part of that dialog contains several tabs. Click on the **Properties** tab (see Figure 2.11).

4. Click on the **Add** button.

5. Select our custom controller **GetSalesOrderCust** and click **OK**.

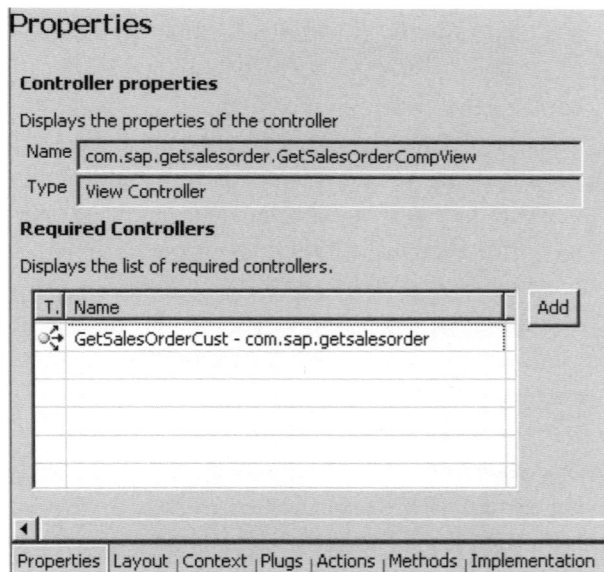

Figure 2.11 View and Connected Custom Controller

Building the View Context

We now have to build up the context of the view in order to access the model data from the view.

1. Open the nodes **WDGetSalesOrder · Web Dynpro · Web Dynpro Components · GetSalesOrderComp · Views**.

2. Open the context menu and select the view **GetSalesOrderCompView**, then select **Edit**. Alternatively, you can double-click on the view.

3. A dialog opens in the right-hand part of the screen in which you can edit the view; click on the **Context** tab

4. Open the context menu of the **Context** node and then select **New · Model Node**.

5. The new node is assigned the name "BAPI_SALESORDER_GETLIST_INPUT". Click on **Finish**.

6. Click on the context menu of the new node **BAPI_SALESORDER_GETLIST_INPUT** and select **Edit Context Mapping**.

7. In the next dialog, click on the **BAPI_SALESORDER_GETLIST_INPUT** node, and then click **Next**.

8. Select all nodes provided (**Output · Return**, **Output · Sales_Order** as well as **Customer_Number**, **Document_Date**, **Document_Date_To** and **Sales_Organization**). Click on **Finish**.

9. Select **Save all Metadata** from the menu bar to save the context.

We have now successfully built a context for our view (see Figure 2.12).

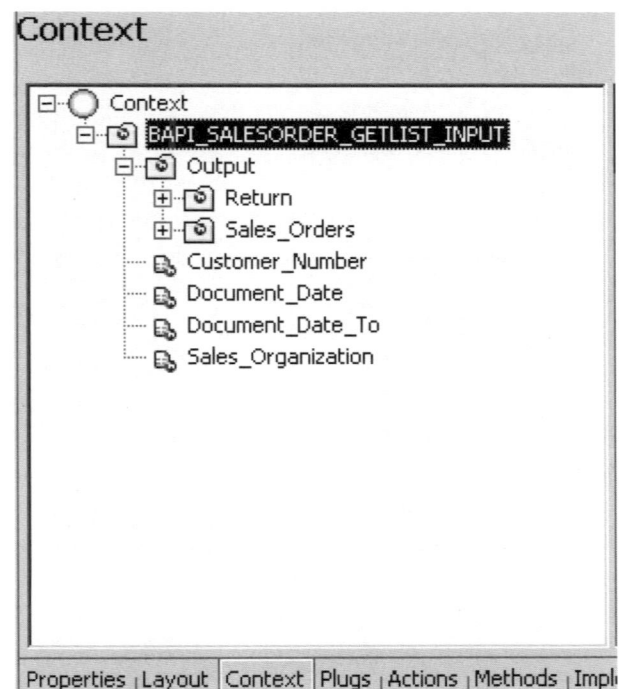

Figure 2.12 Building Context in the View

Adding an Action

For starting the search for sales orders, we want to integrate a button in the user interface that is linked to an action. An action is essentially an event handler linked to a UI item.

1. If you're still in the view from the previous step, you can proceed with Step 3 now, otherwise open the nodes **WDGetSalesOrder · Web Dynpro · Web Dynpro Components · GetSalesOrderComp · Views**.
2. Right-click on the **GetSalesOrderCompView** view and select **Edit**.
3. A dialog opens in the right-hand part of the screen in which you can edit the view. Then select the **Action** tab.
4. Click on **New**.
5. A new dialog opens in which you can enter the **Action properties**. Enter the value "GetOrderList" in the **Name** and **Text** fields and click on **Finish** (see Figure 2.13).
6. Click on **Save all Metadata** in the menu bar.

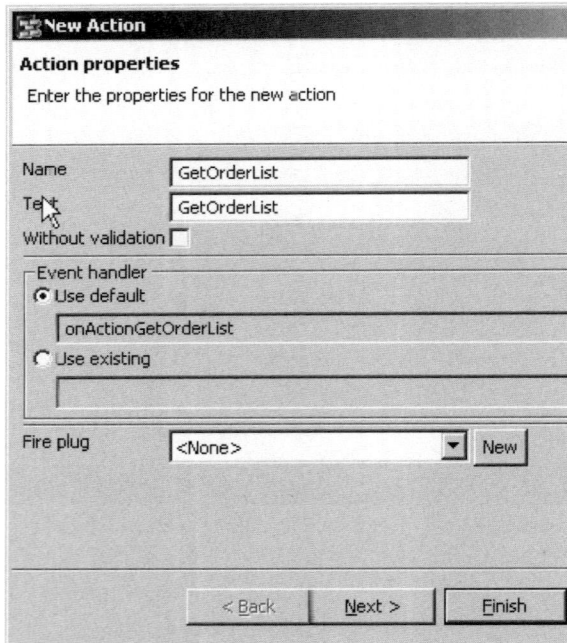

Figure 2.13   Entering Action Properties

Once you have added the action, you will notice two things: A new entry has been added to the list of actions of the controller, and, at the same time, a new method has been generated.

If you click on the **Implementation** tab and scroll to the end of the generated code, you will see that the method `onActionGetOrderList` has been generated.

2.2   Designing the User Interface of the Sales Order List

Before we start constructing the user interface, we should first consider its layout. As mentioned above, we want ultimately to be able to display the search options and the result list on-screen. It would certainly help if we could hide the search options whenever we want to. This way, more space would become available on the screen for the result list.

Such a function is provided by the UI element **Tray**. To design a uniform user interface, we'll also embed the sales order list in a **Tray**.

1. If you're still in the view from the previous step, you can proceed with Step 3 now, otherwise open the nodes **WDGetSalesOrder · Web Dynpro · Web Dynpro Components · GetSalesOrderComp · Views**.
2. Select the view **GetSalesOrderCompView** from the context menu, and then select **Edit**.
3. A dialog opens in the right-hand part of the screen in which you can edit the view. Click on the **Layout** tab.
4. The **Outline** dialog opens in the lower left-hand part of the screen. If that's not the case, you can also open it via **Window · Open View · Outline**.
5. The **Outline** dialog displays the **RootUIElementContainer** and the text element **DefaultTextView** underneath. Open the context menu of **DefaultTextView** and select **Delete** to delete the element. The **DefaultTextView** element is created automatically, but we won't need it.
6. Now you can create the trays. Open the context menu of **RootUIElementContainer** and select **Insert Child**.
7. Enter "TraySearchOptions" as **Id** for the new element; select **Tray** for the **Type**.
8. Open the newly created element in the **Outline View** and click on the subordinate element **TraySearchOptions_Header**. Open the context menu of **TraySearchOptions_Header** and select **Properties**. The properties are now displayed in lower right-hand part of the screen.

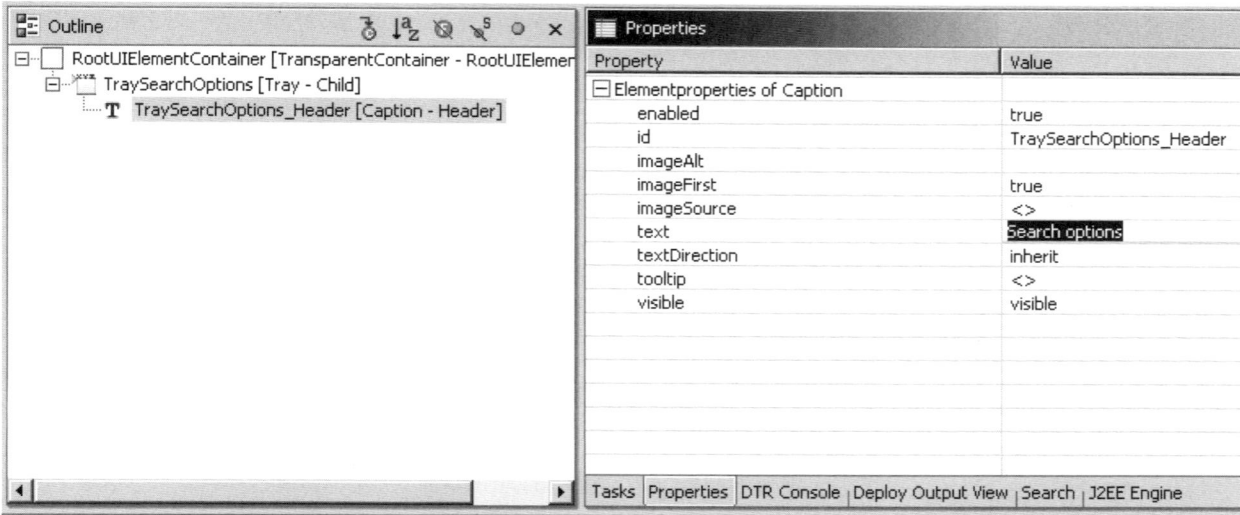

Figure 2.14 Element Properties

9. Click on the **Value** of the **text** field and enter the text "Search options" (see Figure 2.14). When you leave the input field you'll see that the header of the tray you just entered is displayed now.

10. Create another tray, and call it "TrayResults". You should also create this tray as a subordinate element of **RootUIElementContainer**. You can do this by using the **Insert Child** menu item. For the tray header enter the text "Sales order list" (see Figure 2.15).

11. Save the result via **Save all Metadata** in the menu bar.

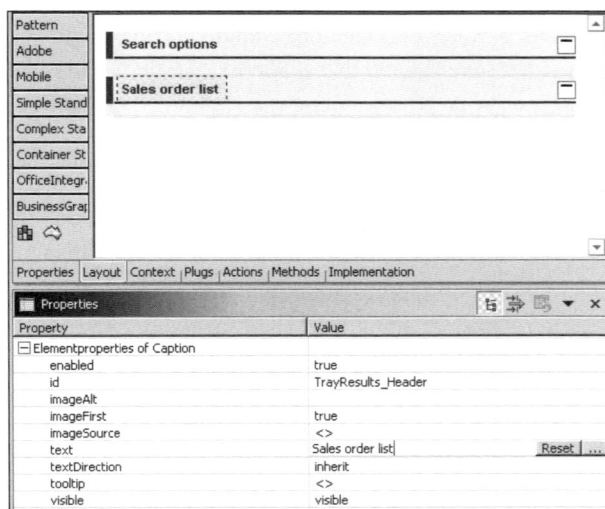

Figure 2.15 View with two Trays

In the next step, we'll create the input fields for the search options.

1. Click on the **TraySearchOptions** node in the **Outline View**, open the context menu, and select **Properties**.

2. In the tray properties, reset the **Layout** value from **FlowLayout** to **GridLayout**. Set the **colCount** value to "2". These two values enable you to use a grid in order to split the screen into several parts and place elements in specific locations.

3. In the following steps, you should create all the elements listed in Table 2.1 as children of **TraySearchOptions**. To do that, you should always use the context menu of **TraySearchOptions** and the menu item **Insert Child**. Apart from that, the procedure is the same as the one for creating the trays. Figure 2.16 shows the layout after integrating the search options.

Id	Type	Property Values
LabelCustomer_Number	Label	**text**: Customer number
InputCustomer_Number	InputField	**value**: Customer_Number*

Table 2.1 List of Input Fields

---

* The values of the input fields are displayed in a form shorter than the original. The long versions of the field names actually always start with "BAPI_SALESORDER_GETLIST_INPUT." This is where the mapping between the user interface and the context occurs. You can select the values from the Context Viewer, which you start with the ... button.

Id	Type	Property Values
LabelSales_ Organization	Labe	**text**: Sales organization
InputSales_ Organization	InputField	**value**: SalesOrganization
LabelDocument_ Date	Label	**text**: From date
InputDocument_ Date	InputField	**value**: Document_Date
LabelDocument_ Date_To	Label	**text**: To date
InputDocument_ Date_To	InputField	**value**: Document_Date_To
ButtonGetOrder- List	Buttor	**text**: Get order list **onAction**: GetOrderList

Table 2.1 List of Input Fields (cont.)

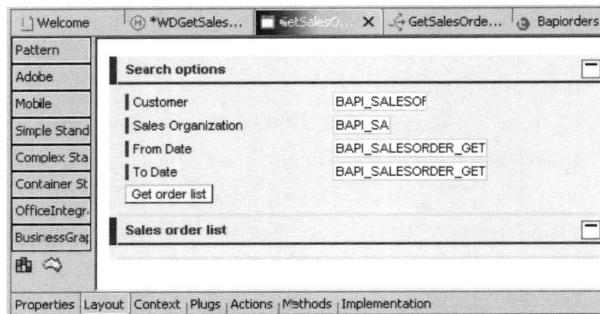

Figure 2.16 Layout After Integrating the Search Options

Not only do we want to enter the selection options, but we also want to see the result. For this purpose, we'll use a UI element called **Table**. In the following steps, we'll create the corresponding UI element, link it to the results table, and define the fields to be displayed. The results table is displayed right below the search options.

1. Click on the **TrayResults** node in the **Outline View**, open the context menu and select **Insert Child**.
2. The **ID** of the new element is **TableSalesOrderList**, the **Type** is **Table**. Click on **Finish**.
3. In the **datasource** field, open the Context Viewer by clicking on the **...** button, then open the node **BAPI_SALESORDER_GETLIST_INPUT · Output** and click on **Sales_Orders**. Confirm this by clicking **OK**. That way we have provided our table with a data source.

4. We still have to define the fields of the results table that should be output. To do this, open the context menu of **TableSalesOrderList** in the **Outline View**, and select **Create Binding**.
5. Select the following fields and click on **Next**:
   ▸ **Sd_Doc** (sales and distribution document number)
   ▸ **Itm_Number** (item number of the sales and distribution document)
   ▸ **Material** (material number)
   ▸ **Short_Text** (short text for the sales order item)
   ▸ **Doc_Date** (document date)
   ▸ **Req_Qty** (order quantity)
   ▸ **Base_Uom** (base unit of measure)
   ▸ **Purch_No_C** (PO number of the customer)
6. All the selected fields are then displayed for you to double-check, and you can still change the sequence in which they are listed. To do that, click into the relevant row and move it by using the arrow buttons on the right-hand side. If the list is not in the order mentioned above, then change the order accordingly (see Figure 2.17), and click on **Finish**.

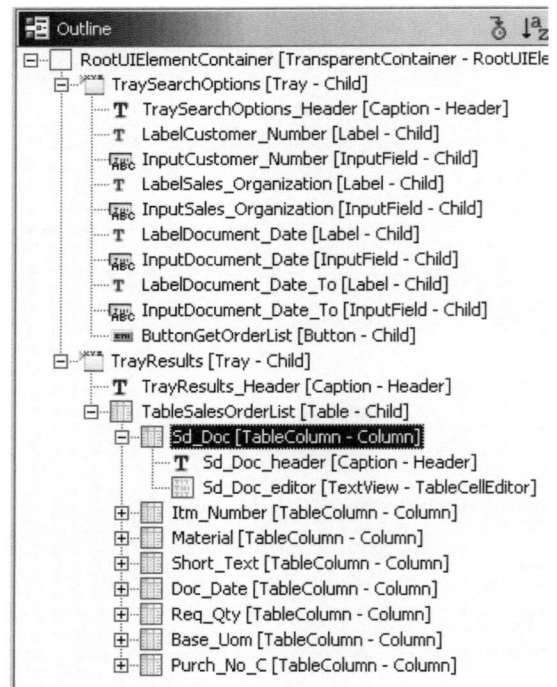

Figure 2.17 Outline View after Creating the UI Elements

We created the project, imported a model, created a custom controller, and designed the UI, all this without writing a single line of code. That's the nature of Web Dynpro applications. You can write large applications with very little code as long as you act within the standard scenarios. However, we can't do without code entirely.

Implementing the GetOrderList Event Handler

In our view GetSalesOrderCompView we have created an action (GetOrderList) that was linked to the input button **Get order list**. We now have to implement the function that the application should execute when this action is triggered.

1. Click on the **Implementation** tab of the view GetSalesOrderCompView.
2. Find the generated method onActionGetOrderList and insert the code from Listing 2.1. Make sure you only add your code in places marked with @@begin and @@end. Otherwise, it can get lost when new methods are generated.

Basically, the added coding consists of one line specifying that the executeBAPI_SALESORDER_GETLIST method is called from the custom controller GetSales-

OrderCust. At that point, you can see how the view is linked to the controller.

Implementing the Custom Controller GetSalesOrderCust

The biggest part of the work is done in the custom controller GetSalesOrderCust. Here, an instance is assigned to the new elements, and the Business Application Programming Interface (BAPI) is called. You can implement the custom controller by performing the following steps:

1. Open the nodes **WDGetSalesOrder · Web Dynpro · Web Dynpro Components · GetSalesOrderComp · Custom Controllers**.
2. Open the context menu of the controller GetSalesOrderCust and select **Edit**.
3. A dialog opens in the right-hand part of the screen in which you can edit the controller. Click on the **Implementation** tab.
4. Find the wdDoInit() method and insert the code shown in Listing 2.2.

The wdDoInit method is always called when the custom controller GetSalesOrderCust is initialized. We create

```
public void ¬
onActionGetOrderList(com.sap.tc.webdynpro.progmodel.api.IWDCustomEvent wdEvent )
{
  //@@begin onActionGetOrderList(ServerEvent)
  wdThis.wdGetGetSalesOrderCustController().executeBAPI_SALESORDER_GETLIST();
  //@@end
}
```
Listing 2.1 onActionGetOrderList

```
public void wdDoInit()
{
  //@@begin wdDoInit()
  // Create a new element from context node BAPI_SALESORDER_GETLIST_INPUT
  Bapi_Salesorder_Getlist_Input input = new Bapi_Salesorder_Getlist_Input();
  wdContext.nodeBAPI_SALESORDER_GETLIST_INPUT().bind(input);
  //@@end
}
```
Listing 2.2 Initialization

```
public void executeBAPI_SALESORDER_GETLIST( )
{
  //@@begin executeBAPI_SALESORDER_GETLIST()
  try{
    // Call function module BAPI_SALESORDER_GETLIST
    wdContext.currentBAPI_SALESORDER_GETLIST_INPUTElement().modelObject().execute();
  }
  catch (Exception ex)
  {
    // If an exception is returned, output the stack
    ex.printStackTrace();
  }
  //Synchronize the data in the context with the model data
  wdContext.nodeOutput().invalidate();
  //@@end
}
```

Listing 2.3 Calling the BAPI

a new instance of the context node BAPI_SALESORDER_GETLIST_INPUT and bind it.

The BAPI is to be called in the executeBAPI_SALESORDER_GETLIST method. Insert Listing 2.3 into the method.

In Listing 2.3, the function module BAPI_SALESORDER_GETLIST is called in the method executeBAPI_SALESORDER_GETLIST. The result is then synchronized with the model.

Once you have inserted the code, open the context menu in the code area and select **Source · Organize Imports**. This way, all required imports are transferred automatically.

In the current state of the code, the imports shown in Listing 2.4 are inserted automatically, if they don't exist yet.

Note on Working with the Code Editor

You can format the code at any time by using the **Source · Format** menu item. This helps to improve the readability of the code. If you wait a couple of seconds after entering the object name and the dot, all methods and sub-objects are displayed. This saves you some typing work and it avoids entering typos.

Creating an Application

Before we can run a first test on our application we must create another application which our program runs on.

1. To do that, open the nodes **WDGetSalesOrder · Web Dynpro**.

2. Right-click on the **Applications** node, and select **Create Application** from the context menu.

3. A dialog opens in which you can maintain the **Application Properties**. The **Name** of the application is WDGetSalesOrder, and the **Package** in which we want to store the application is "com.sap.wdgetsalesorder". Click **Next**.

4. As we have already created the components, you can select **Use existing component** in the **Referenced Web Dynpro Component** dialog, and then click **Next**.

5. Since we created only one component, the input fields in the next dialog should automatically contain the correct values (see Figure 2.18).

```
import com.sap.getsalesorder.wdp.IPrivateGetSalesOrderCust;
import com.sap.wdgetsalesorder.models.bapi_salesorder_getlist.¬
Bapi_Salesorder_Getlist_Input;
```

Listing 2.4 Automatically Generated Imports

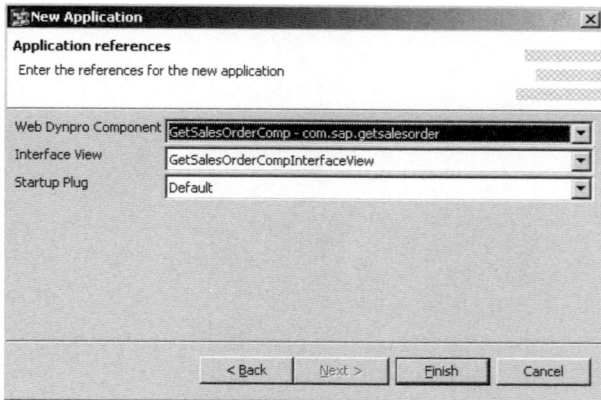

Figure 2.18 Application References

6. In the **Web Dynpro Component** field, the component GetSalesOrderComp is provided, while in the **Interface View** field the "GetSalesOrderCompInterfaceView" view is suggested. Confirm these values by clicking on **Finish**.

At this point, we have created all required components and implemented the entire necessary code so that we can deploy the project now.

Building, Deploying, Configuring and Testing the Application

Before we start deploying the project, we want to create a rebuild of it so that all the required files of the project are rebuilt. To do that, open the context menu of the top project node, **WDGetSalesOrder,** and select **Rebuild Project**. Then select the **Deploy** command from the same context menu which transfers the entire project to the server.

Until now, we haven't specified any R/3 system on which the BAPI is to be called. When we created the model, we filled the following two fields with data: We linked the field **Default logical system name for model**

instances with the logical system name WD_MODEL-DATA_DEST, whereas the field **Default logical system name for RFC metadata** was linked to the logical system name WD_RFC_METADATA_DEST. Before running our application, we must assign actual systems to those logical system names.

At this stage, we assume that the *System Landscape Directory* (SLD) has been completely configured. If that's not the case, you must first configure the SLD as described in Section 5.1.

1. Open the home page of your SAP J2EE engine *http://<host>:<port>/index.html* (e.g. *http://localhost:50000/index.html*).

2. Click on **Web Dynpro**.

3. Select **Content Administrator** in the dialog that opens.

4. If you haven't logged on to the item yet, you will now be prompted to authenticate yourself. Log on with a user ID that has the relevant authorizations; if you're unsure, you should log on as an administrator.

5. Open the tree **Deployed Content · local · local/WDGetSalesOrder** in the left-hand pane of the screen.

6. If you click on the node **local/WDGetSalesOrder**, the system displays the details of our application on the right. Click on the **JCO Connections** tab (see Figure 2.19).

7. Now we have to create the connection to the R/3 systems. To do that, click on the **Create** button next to WD_MODELDATA_DEST. In the lower part of the **JCO Connections** tab, a wizard opens that guides you through the creation of a new **JCo Destination** (see Figure 2.20). The data you then have to enter depends on your system landscape so that the following data is only an example.

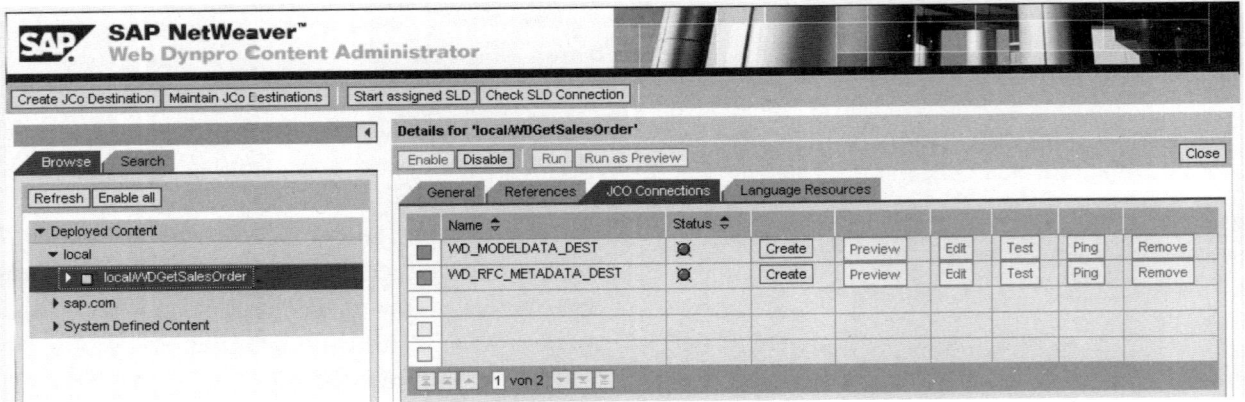

Figure 2.19 Web Dynpro Content Administrator

8. In the first step (**General Data**), you must enter the client of your R/3 system. You can copy all other entries. Click **Next**.

9. You next must specify the **J2EE Cluster**. Don't change any of the suggested settings and click on the **Next** button.

10. Mistakes are often made during the configuration of the **Destination Type** so that the application can't be executed.
It's not possible to read the metadata through a **Single Server Connection**, which means that at least for the JCo Destination WD_RFC_METADATA_DEST we must go through a message server. For the

JCo Destination WD_MODELDATA_DEST, click on **Application Data**, but keep the **Destination Type** setting at **Load-balanced Connection**.
For WD_RFC_METADATA_DEST select **Dictionary Meta Data**. In this case, you can't change the **Destination Type**. Click **Next**.

11. Depending on your selections in the previous step, select application or message server respectively. The servers must have been configured in the SLD (see also Section 5.1). For the message server you must also specify the logon group. If necessary, you should maintain the SAProuter string.

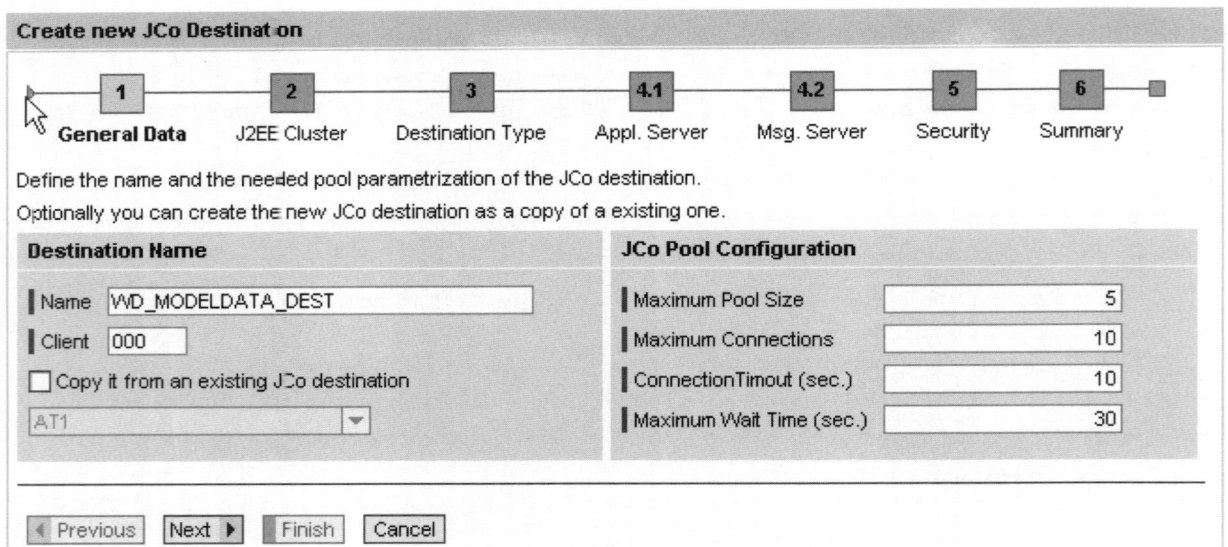

Figure 2.20 Creating a New JCo Destination

Tip

There are versions in which this last process doesn't function without a problem. That is to say, although you check the **Use SAProuter** checkbox, the **SAProuter String** field won't open. If that happens, select **Use SAProuter**, click **Next**, and then click **Previous**. Now you can enter a value in the **SAProuter String** field. Click **Next**.

12. In the **Security** step, you must enter a user name and password. Click **Next**.
13. Check your entries in the **Summary** and click on **Finish**.

Repeat this procedure for WD_RFC_METADATA_DEST. The traffic lights for the JCo Connections should now be green. But don't let yourself be fooled: The green traffic lights merely mean that the JCo Connections have been created; they don't mean that the connection was created correctly.

However, you can check that by clicking on the **Test** button. Only if the test is successful for both connections can you execute your application. The connection test message is displayed at the bottom of the screen, and you might have to scroll down to be able to see it.

Starting the Application

The time has come: Go back into SAP NetWeaver Developer Studio and open the tree **WDGetSalesOrder · Web Dynpro · Applications · WDGetSalesOrder**.

Click on the node **WDGetSalesOrder**, open the context menu, and select **Run**. The application starts (see Figure 2.21). Enter a valid customer number and sales organization, and click on **Get Order List**. You can retrieve the existing customer numbers and sales organizations from the respective transactions in the SD module of the connected R/3 system. As we already mentioned, we connected an IDES system 4.7 for our example.

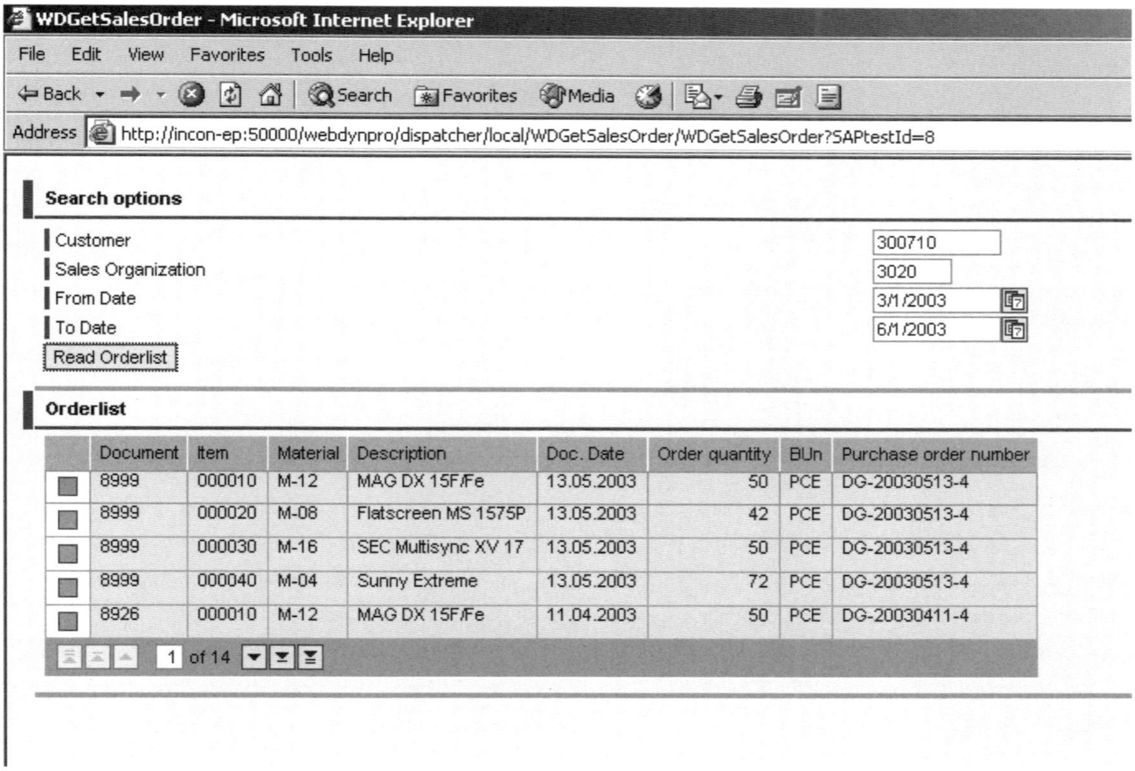

Figure 2.21 First Web Dynpro Application

2.3   Portal Integration of the Sales Order List

In the next step we want to integrate our new application as an *iView* into SAP Enterprise Portal 6.0.

1. To do that, you must log on to SAP Enterprise Portal. To be able to perform the following steps, you must at least have content-administrator rights.
2. Select **Content Administration · Portal Content** and open the tree **Portal Content**.
3. If you don't have a folder for your own applications yet, open the context menu of the *Portal Content* folder and select **New · Folder** (see Figure 2.22).

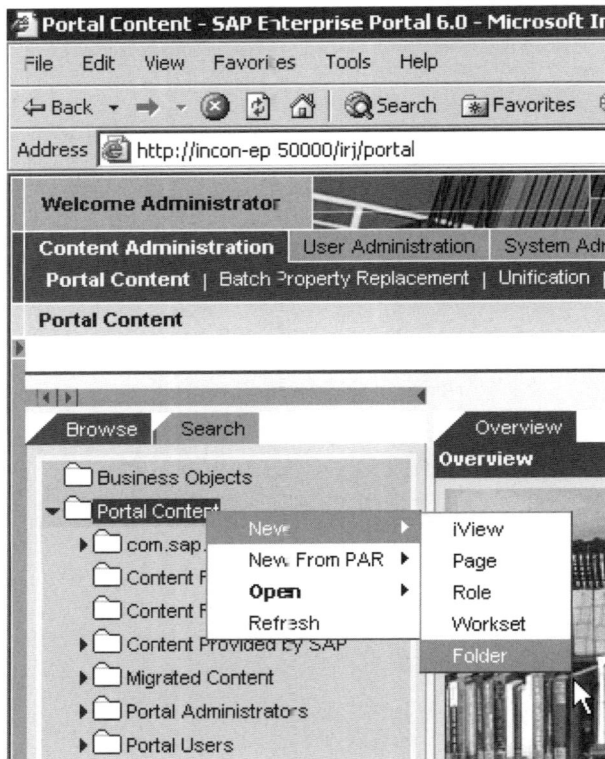

Figure 2.22   Creating a New Folder in the Portal Content

4. The folder wizard opens in the right-hand part of the screen. Enter "MyContent" into the **Folder name** and **Folder ID** fields, and click on **Finish**.
5. Select the **Close wizard** option in the dialog that opens and click **OK**.
6. Proceed in the same manner to create an *iViews* and a *Roles* folder as subfolders of *MyContent*.
7. Create a *Sales orders* folder as a subfolder of *iViews*.

Creating an iView

Web applications can be integrated into a portal via iViews. For this purpose, various templates are available. In the following steps we'll create an iView through which we can call the Web Dynpro application we previously created.

1. Open the context menu of the **Sales orders** folder and select **New · iView**. A wizard opens. In the first step you must select an appropriate template, in our example that's **iView SAP-Web-Dynpro**. Click on **Next**.
2. Assign the **iView Name** "Order List" and the **iView ID** "WDGetOrderList". The **Master Language** is **English** (see Figure 2.23). Click on **Next**.

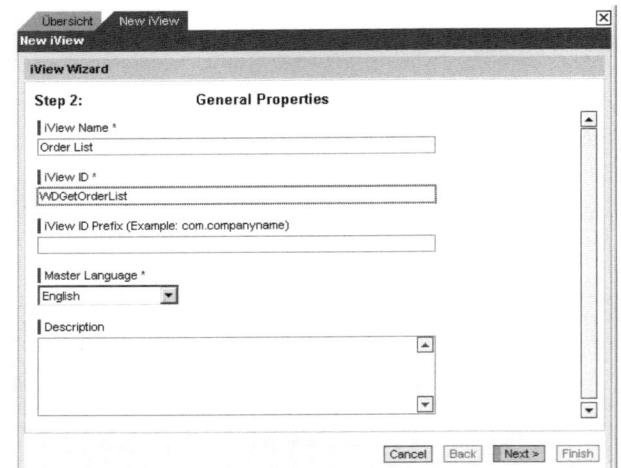

Figure 2.23   General iView Properties

3. Select the application variant **JAVA** and click on **Next**.
4. In the next step you must maintain the application parameters of the Web Dynpro application (see Figure 2.24). If the Web Dynpro runtime environment is located on the same system as the portal, select the **SAP_LocalSystem** entry in the **System** field; otherwise select the corresponding system. Enter "local/WDGetSalesOrder" in the **WebDynproNamespace** field, and "WDGetSalesOrder" in the **Application name** field. Click on **Next**.
5. The system displays another overview of the iView to be created. Check the **Open for editing when wizard completes** checkbox, and click on **Finish**.

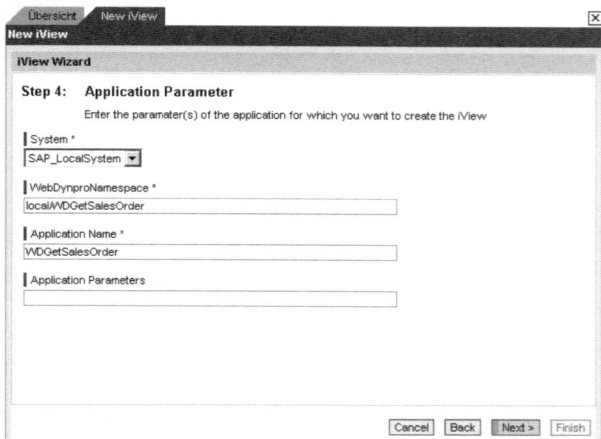

Figure 2.24 iView Application Parameters

The creation of an iView for our application is now completed, and we're now in the processing details view. Here you can take a look at what you've done up until now by clicking on the **Preview** button.

To be able to call the iView from the menu, we must assign it to a role which in turn must be assigned to various users.

Creating a Role

There are at least two groups that are going to use our portal: employees and customers. We want to control the accesses of those two groups by using different roles.

1. For this reason, open the tree **Portal Content · My-Content**, then open the context menu of **Roles** and select **New · Role**. In the role wizard, enter the value "Employee" in the **Role name** and **Role ID** fields for the first role we want to create.

2. Your entries then will be summarized and you can confirm them by clicking on the **Finish** button. Finally, select **Open the object for editing** and click **OK**.

3. To be able to access the iViews of the role through the main navigation, the role must be marked as an entry point. Therefore you should set the **Entry Point** attribute in the properties editor to **Yes**, and then save the role. As we won't be needing the role for a while, you can close it now.

Create the **Customer** role in the same way.

Assigning an iView to the Role

In the following step we want to assign our iView **Order List** to the **Employee** role.

1. Open the context menu of the **Employee** role and select **Open · Object** (see Figure 2.25).

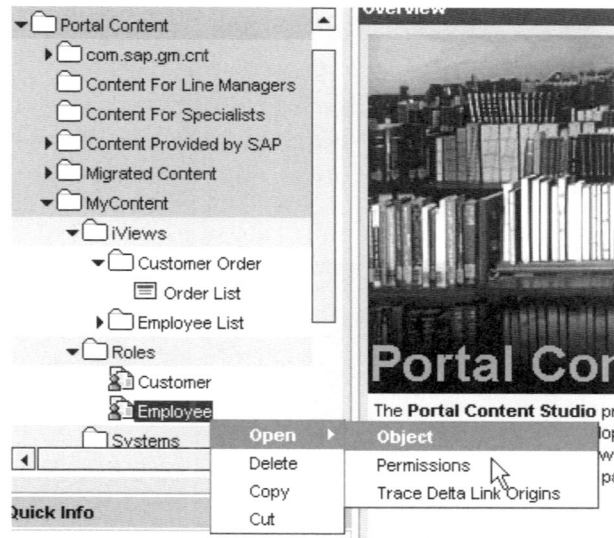

Figure 2.25 Opening the Employee Role

2. In the right-hand pane of the screen the system now displays the role details. Then open the context menu of the iView **Sales Order List** and select **Add iView to Role · Delta Link**.

In the delta link process, the properties of the original iView are adopted and also used for later changes to the original iView. In contrast, the properties of the iView in a copy process are copied and remain unchanged even if the original iView is changed.

Assigning a Role to a User

Finally we want to assign the **Employee** role to a user. To do that, you must be logged on with a user ID that has the relevant administrator rights.

1. Select **User administration · Roles**. The **Search** dialog opens in the lower part of the screen. Enter the user name you want to assign the **Employee** role to, select **User** from the dropdown box and click on the **Start** button. If you haven't maintained many users in your system yet, you can also leave the first field blank.

2. Click on **Edit** for the respective user.
3. The assigned roles are displayed in the upper right-hand part of the screen. In the lower right-hand part, you can search for existing roles that can be added to the user. Find the Employee role, highlight it, and add it to the user (see Figure 2.26). Remember to save your entries.

Once you have added the role to the user, you can view the result. Log on to the portal as an employee (see Figure 2.27).

2.4   Displaying Order Details

In the preceding sections we created an application that enables a portal user to view a list of sales orders. We now want to fine-tune the application and add another option: Clicking on a document number causes the order details to be displayed in a separate window (see Figure 2.28).

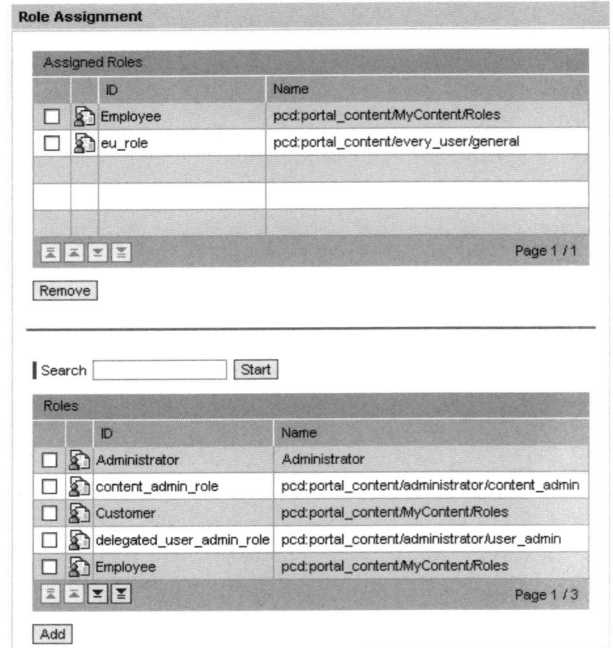

Figure 2.26   Employee Role Added

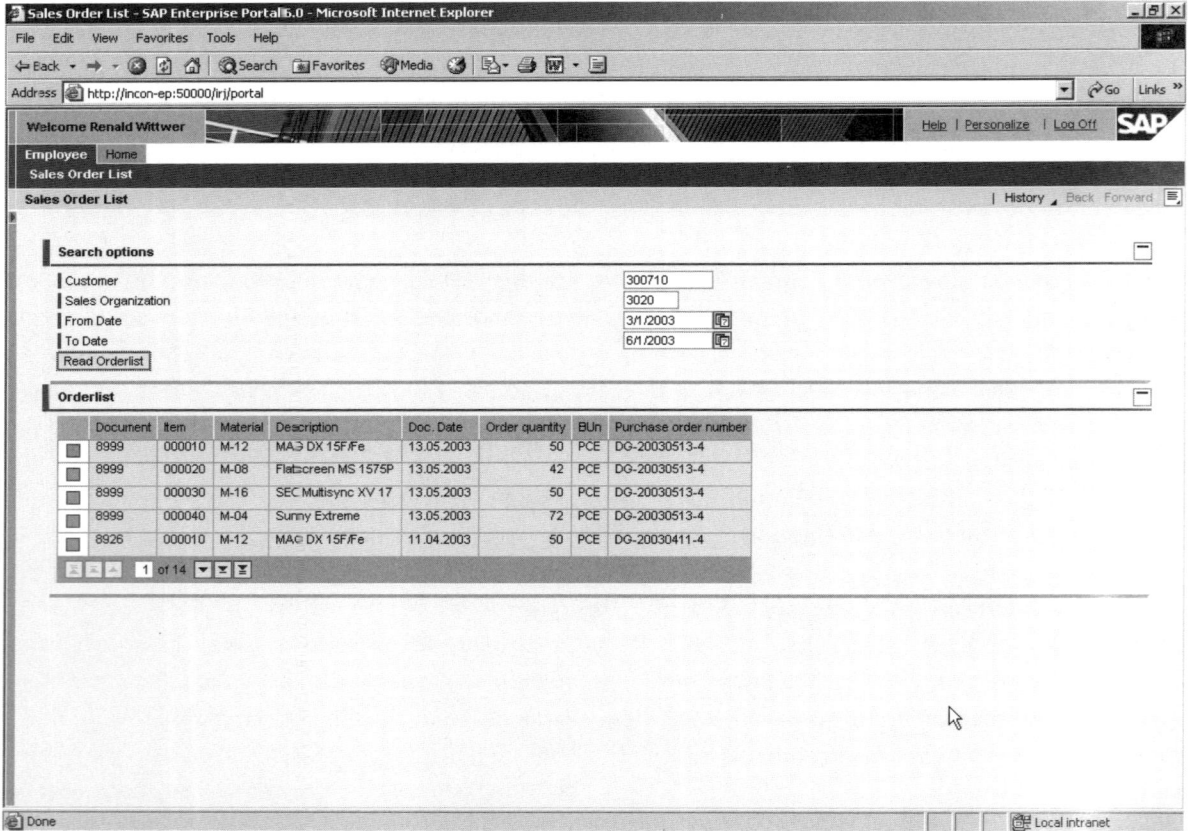

Figure 2.27   Sales Order List in the Portal

From a technical point of view we have two options: either develop an entirely new application, or enhance the existing one. In terms of the subject matter, the order list and order details have much in common, so it is advisable to enhance the existing application.

Finding the BAPI and Creating a Wrapper

For the order details, we need a separate function module that reads additional details of a selected order.

One of the biggest challenges in developing applications in the SAP environment is to find the right BAPIs. The success or failure of a project depends very much on this action, so we thought it might be useful to describe it in further detail here.

A useful starting point for finding the right BAPI is the *BAPI Explorer*. It has been available since Release 4.6A and is called via SAP GUI using Transaction BAPI. The BAPI Explorer provides a good overview of all BAPIs that exist in the *Business Object Repository* (BOR). You can change the display of that overview and either view the hierarchical location of the corresponding object type or interface type, or you can view them in alphabetical order. Figure 2.29, for instance, displays the function module BAPI_SALESORDER_GETLIST we used in Section 2.1.

Another option for obtaining information on existing BAPIs is to use the *SAP notes*. Via *http://service.sap.com/notes* you have access to all SAP notes. You only need a user ID in SAP Service Marketplace. For example, Note 93091 contains valuable information on BAPIs in the sales and distribution module SD.

Another option is to develop your own RFC-enabled modules. If the required functionality isn't provided by the standard BAPIs, the only way out is to program them yourself. But, before you develop your own function modules, you should accurately check if there isn't any BAPI available that provides the functionality you need. Once you have decided to use modules you have programmed, you must ensure their robustness, which in this context means that your developments should be as release-independent as possible. You can, for instance, try to use standard SAP components within a function module.

In our application, we want to read the detail data of a sales order. SAP Note 93091 contains the decisive hint that we can use the function module BAPISDORDER_GETDETAILEDLIST for that. This function module provides exactly the data we require, although there's one big drawback about it: It provides more data than needed.

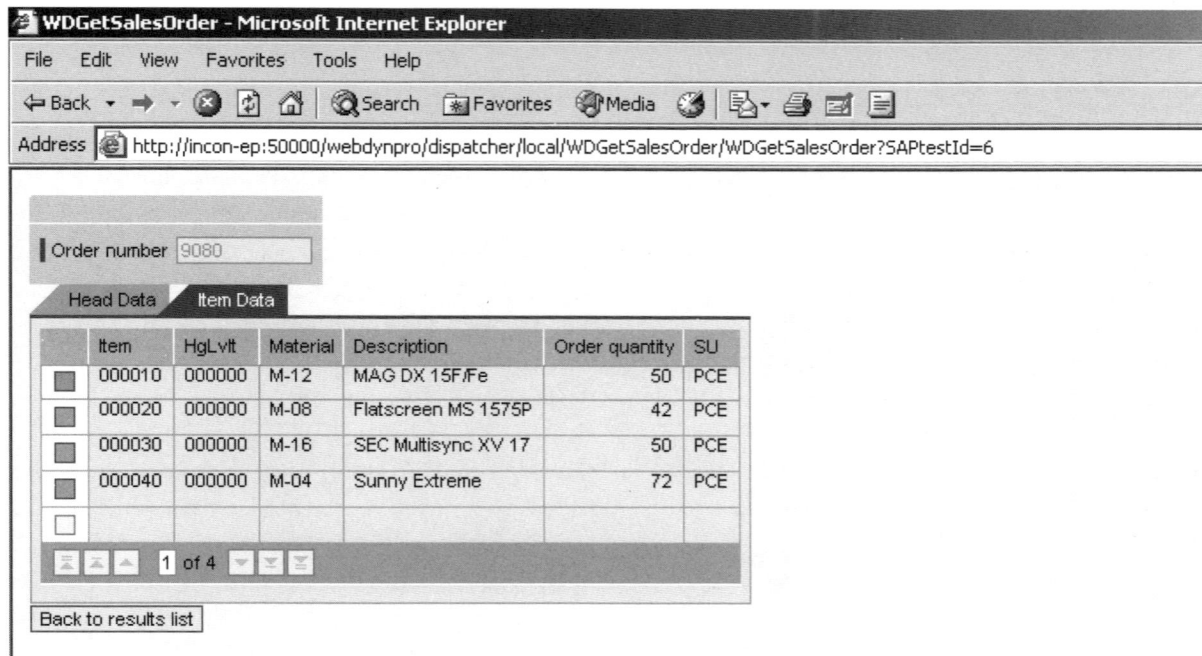

Figure 2.28 Order Details

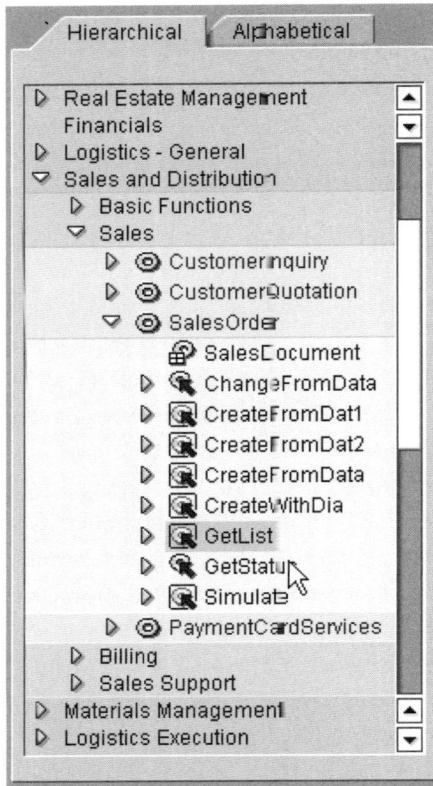

Figure 2.29 BAPI Explorer

As complex structures result in a complex model, this could unnecessarily increase the size of our project or even affect the system performance. Therefore it is a common practice to build *wrappers* around a BAPI or a function module. A wrapper can call one or more function modules and reduce the data to be read to the amount of data needed. We'll implement such a wrapper in the following steps.

1. Logon to your SAP system via SAP GUI.
2. Call Transaction SE37.
3. Create the function module Z_SDORDER_GETDETAILEDLIST by entering the function module name and clicking on **Create**.
4. Assign the new function module to a function group and describe the functionality in the short text, for instance "Wrapper for function module BAPIS-DORDER_GETDETAILEDLIST".
5. Select a package in which you want to summarize your own developments.

6. Check the process type **Remote-enabled module** in the **Attributes** tab. This ensures that the function module can be called externally.
7. As we don't only want to simplify the outbound parameters but also the inbound parameters, we should directly transfer the document number to be read to the wrapper. To do that, click on the **Import** tab, maintain the parameter name "I_SD_DOC" of the "VBELN" type, and check the **Pass** value (see Figure 2.30).

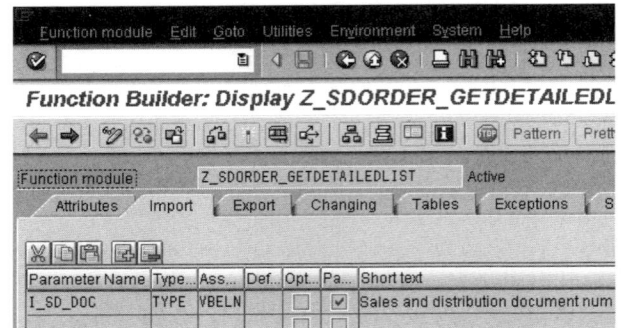

Figure 2.30 Import Parameters for our Wrapper

8. We now want to have the system return the header and item data of the document as result data. In order to keep the example simple, we'll use the original structures. Naturally, it would be possible to define our own structures in accordance with the required data.
   Moreover, you could also import the table ORDER_HEADERS_OUT as a structure into the export parameters as we can only read one document; this facilitates the access in the subsequent programs.
9. Go to the **Tables** tab and maintain the table parameters as shown in Figure 2.31.
10. Go to the **Source Text** tab and import the source code from Listing 2.5.
11. Save and activate the function module.

As you can see, it's not difficult to develop a wrapper. You must first define the required transfer variables, and the document numbers to be read are transferred as a list. Then you add the document number to be read to the document numbers list.

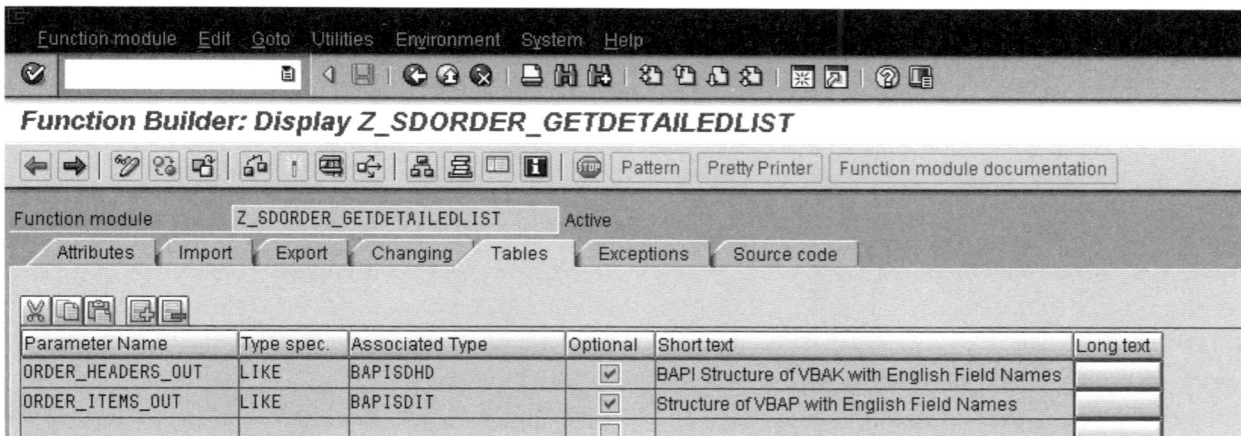

Figure 2.31 Imported Header and Item Data of our Wrapper

To optimize system performance and to reduce the amount of data, you must activate all areas to be read. We only want to read the header and item data, which means we have to activate those two areas. Finally, the BAPI is called. Here we'll use the same event structures as the original function module so that we can transfer the read data directly into our export variables.

Creating a Model

In the next step you'll create a model of Z_SDORDER_GETDETAILEDLIST. As we have already described this step in Section 2.1, we won't describe it in further detail here. Figure 2.32 shows the values you must enter for importing the model.

```
FUNCTION z_sdorder_getdetailedlist.
*"----------------------------------------------------------------
*"*"Local interface:
*"  IMPORTING
*"     VALUE(I_SD_DOC) TYPE  VBELN
*"  TABLES
*"      ORDER_HEADERS_OUT STRUCTURE  BAPISDHD OPTIONAL
*"      ORDER_ITEMS_OUT STRUCTURE  BAPISDIT OPTIONAL
*"----------------------------------------------------------------
  DATA: i_bapi_view   TYPE order_view,
        sales_documents TYPE TABLE OF sales_key,
        wa_sales_documents LIKE LINE OF sales_documents.
  wa_sales_documents-vbeln = i_sd_doc.
  APPEND wa_sales_documents TO sales_documents.
  i_bapi_view-header = 'X'.
  i_bapi_view-item   = 'X'.
  CALL FUNCTION 'BAPISDORDER_GETDETAILEDLIST'
     EXPORTING
       i_bapi_view            = i_bapi_view
     TABLES
```

Listing 2.5 Function Module Z_SDORDER_GETDETAILEDLIST

```
        sales_documents          = sales_documents
        order_headers_out         = order_headers_out
        order_items_out           = order_items_out.
ENDFUNCTION.
```

Listing 2.5 Function Module Z_SDORDER_GETDETAILEDLIST (cont.)

Connecting Model and Component

We must also connect the new model Z_SDORDER_ GETDETAILEDLIST with the component. To do that, proceed as follows.

1. Open the Web Dynpro component **GetSalesOrder-Comp**.
2. Open the context menu of **Used Models** and select **Add**.
3. Select the model **Z_SDORDER_GETDETAILEDLIST** in the selection screen **Selection Needed** and click **OK**.

Enhancing the Custom Controller Context

We want to use the already existing custom controller GetSalesOrderCust to address the new model. For this reason, we must first enhance the context of the custom controller.

1. Open the custom controller **GetSalesOrderCust**.
2. Go to the **Context** tab.
3. Open the context menu of **Context** and select **New · Model Node**, then assign the name Z_SDORDER_ GETDETAILEDLIST to the node. Names of more than 30 characters length can cause platform errors which is why we won't use the suffix _INPUT.
4. Open the context menu of **Z_SDORDER_GETDE-TAILEDLIST** and select **Edit Model Binding ...**
5. Highlight the node **Z_Sdorder_Getdetailedlist_Input** and click on **Next**.

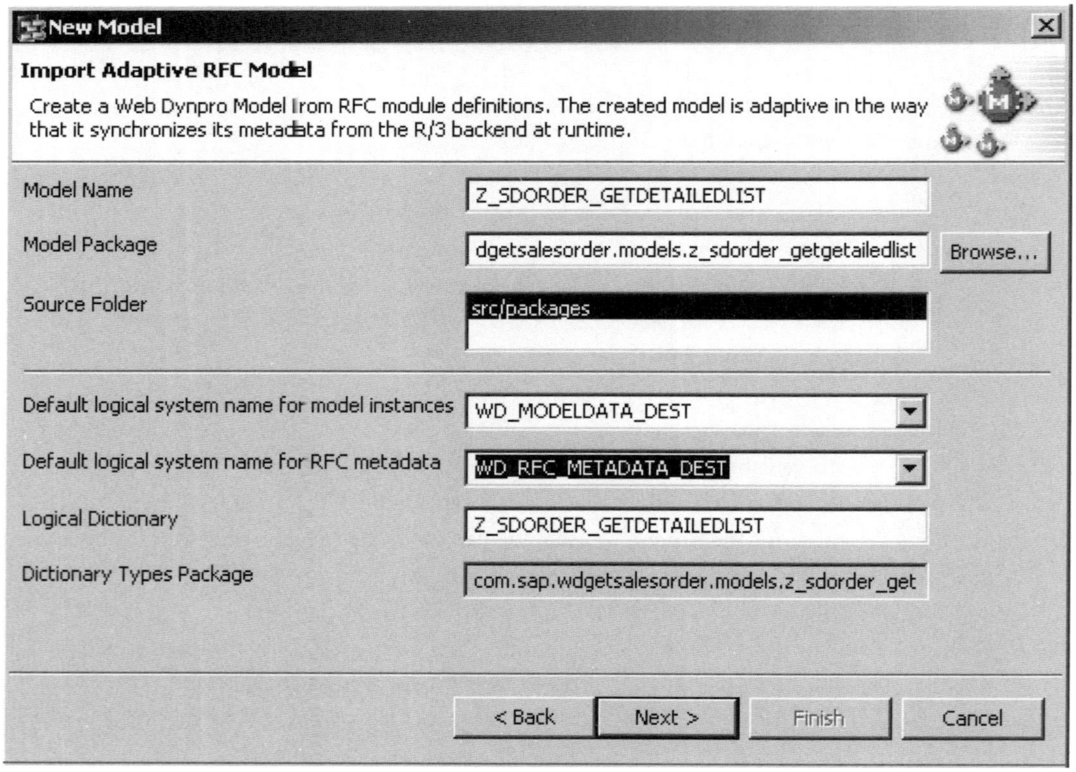

Figure 2.32 Creating a Model of Z_SDORDER_GETDETAILEDLIST

6. We need the import parameter **I_Sd_Doc**: This parameter is used to transfer the order number (sales document number) to be displayed. Highlight this node and select **Finish**.

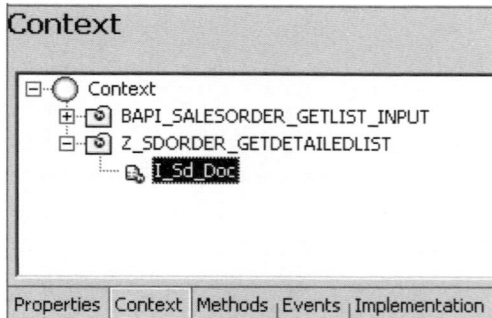

Figure 2.33 Import Parameter I_Sd_Doc

It would also be nice if we could add a node called **Output** to the context BAPISDORDER_GETDETAILEDLIST. The names within nodes must be unique, so we can't use the name "Output" any longer. Do the following to find an alternative.

1. Open the context menu of **Z_SDORDER_GET-DETAILEDLIST** and then select **New · Model Node**.
2. Create a node called "Output_GETDETAILEDLIST".
3. Select **Edit Model Binding ...** in the context menu of the newly created node **Output_GETDETAILEDLIST**.
4. Highlight the node **Z_Sdorder_Getdetailedlist_Output** and click on **Next**.
5. Select **Order_Headers_Out** (header data) and **Order_Items_Out** (order items) and click on **Finish**.
6. Save all metadata.

Thus, in the context of our custom controller GetSalesOrderCust, we have created two nodes of the models' data structures. In addition, we now want to create a separate value attribute which we'll need at a later stage for communication of the views. The order list will write the requested document number for the order detail view into the new value attribute Sd_Doc_Detail, and the order detail view will read this value.

1. Select **New · Value Attribute** in the context menu of **Context**.
2. Assign the name "Sd_Doc_Detail" to the new element. Click on **Finish**.

Defining the Custom Controller Method

We also need a method for our new BAPI, in which the BAPI is executed.

1. In the custom controller **GetSalesOrderCust**, go to the **Methods** tab.
2. Add a new method and call it "executeZ_SDORDER_GETDETAILEDLIST". Here the length restriction to variables of 30 characters applies as well.

Creating a New View for Order Details

The order details are displayed in a separate view which we want to create at this point. When doing this, you can either create a separate view and then assign it to a window or perform both steps at the same time, which is what we're going to do now. In this context, a window represents a kind of container in which several views or view sets can be integrated.

1. Open the context menu of the **GetSalesOrderComp** window and then select **Embed new View**. Click **Next**.
2. The view name is **SalesOrderDetailView**. You can leave all other fields unchanged. Click on **Finish**.

Connecting Custom Controller and View

Our new view SalesOrderDetailView must of course be connected to our custom controller (GetSalesOrderCust) as well.

1. Go to the detail view of **SalesOrderDetailView** and click on the **Properties** tab.
2. Click on the **Add** button.
3. Select our custom controller **GetSalesOrderCust** and click **OK**.

Building View Context

Context that we want to use in the view must first be created and mapped. In the following steps we'll integrate the context of the model Z_SDORDER_GETDETAILEDLIST so that we can easily display the results data of the function module.

1. Click on the **Context** tab.
2. Open the context menu of the **Context** node and then select **New · Model Node**.
3. Assign the name "Z_SDORDER_GETDETAILEDLIST" to the new node. Click on **Finish**.

4. Click on the context menu of the newly created node **Z_SDORDER_GETDETAILEDLIST** and select **Edit Context Mapping**.
5. In the dialog that opens, click on the node **Z_SDORDER_GETDETA LEDLIST** and then on **Next**.
6. Select all fields provided and click on **Finish**.
7. Save the result via **Save all Metadata** in the menu bar.

Creating Actions

To be able to assign the relevant methods to the UI elements at the time they are created, we'll first create the methods and then design the UI layout.

1. Go to the detail view of **SalesOrderDetailView** and click on the **Actions** tab.
2. Create an **Action** called "Back". You can accept all suggested values in the other fields. We'll need this action for returning to the results list.
3. Go to the detail view of **GetSalesOrderCompView** and click on the **Action** tab.
4. Create an **Action** called "GetOrderDetail". Again, you can accept all suggested values in the other fields. We'll need this action for jumping into the detail view of the order.

2.5 Designing the User Interface of the Order Details

Designing user interfaces is a very demanding task, and there are many different points of view on this subject. We don't want to open another discussion about the ergonomics of a user interface, and therefore we simply state that it is up to you to change the UI we provide in this book.

Figure 2.34 displays the planned structure of our page for displaying the order details. The upper part displays the order number which is always displayed, even when you click on the tabs below. In the lower part we'll use tabs for displaying header and item data. Tabs are quite useful because they can be quickly enhanced, in other words, they are very dynamic.

Creating UI Elements

Now we'll create the aforementioned UI elements.

1. Go to the detail view of **SalesOrderDetailView** and click on the **Layout** tab.

Figure 2.34 Structure of the Order Details

2. Delete the automatically generated text element, and open the context menu of **DefaultTextView** in the **Outline** dialog. Then select **Delete**.
3. Create a new element of the **Group** type with the name "GroupHeader" underneath the **RootUIElementContainer** node. We can place the output of the document number inside of this new element. This way we make sure that an enhancement of the header area can easily be performed, especially because it can be done without affecting the layout. Change the **layout** attribute to **GridLayout** and the **colCount** value to "2".
4. Then create a **Label** type element with the name "LabelVbeln" as a subordinate element of **GroupHeader**. Enter the text "Order number" for the **text** attribute which defines the text that will be displayed in the UI.
5. Then create an **InputField** type element with the name "InputVbeln" as another subordinate element of **GroupHeader**. Set the **enabled** attribute to **false**. This way, you can make sure that the input field value can't be changed anymore. Although our design is that of an input field and we can open the field again at a later stage, for the time being we won't have the user access it.

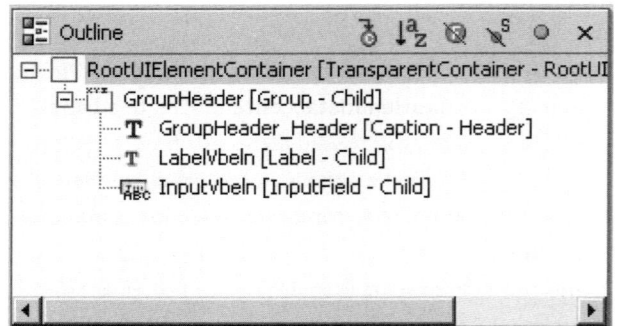

Figure 2.35 Children of GroupHeader

6. Set the **value** attribute to **Z_SDORDER_GETDE-TAILEDLIST.Sales_Documents.Vbeln**.

7. Then you must create a tab called "TabStripOrderDetails" as a child of **RootUIElementContainer**.

8. After that you should create the tabs displayed in Figure 2.36 as children of **TabStripOrderDetails**. To do that, select **Insert Tab** from the context menu; you can change the internal element name provided by the system by overwriting the **Id** attribute.

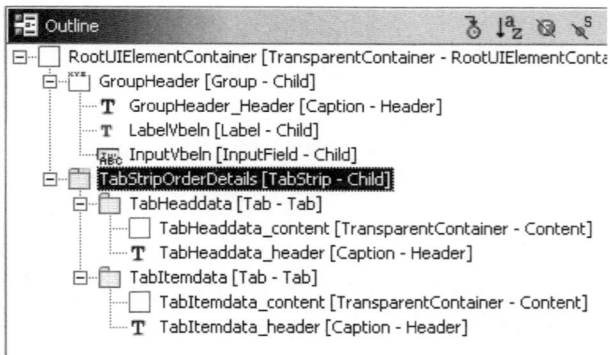

Figure 2.36   Inserting Tabs

9. You can change the tabstrip text displayed, if you go to the **TabXXX_header** subnode. In this case, "XXX" stands for **Headdata** for the header data and **Itemdata** for the item data. Apart from that, you can leave the suggested attribute values unchanged, except for the attributes of **TabHeaddata_content**, where you must select the **GridLayout** setting under **layout** and then set the **colCount** attribute to "2".

Inserting Fields to be Displayed

As the integration of new fields to be displayed always requires the same steps, we'll only display one field in the following sections. Feel free to include more fields if you like.

1. Insert the field "Sales document type" (DOC_TYPE) as a child of **TabHeaddata_content**. Create a **Label** element and an **InputField** element for each field. Overwrite the **text** attribute in the **Label** element with the text you want to display. Set the **enabled** attribute in the **InputField** element to **false,** and assign the corresponding field from the context in the **value** attribute.

2. Make sure that the field to be displayed can be selected from the **Output** node (**Z_SDORDER_GETDE-TAILEDLIST.Output_GETDETAILEDLIST.Order_Headers_Out**).

3. In the **Item Data** tab, we want to display a table that contains the item data. For this reason, we create a **Table** type element under the node **TabItemData_content**. Assign the name "TableOrder_Items_Out" to this element.

4. After creating the **Table** type element, you must assign the data source to it. For tables, this assignment requires a few more steps than for simple data fields. Open the **Properties** of the element **TableOrder_Items_Out** and go to the **dataSource** field. Click on the **Select** button and select the node **Order_Items_Out** from the navigation tree, as shown in Figure 2.37. Then save the metadata.

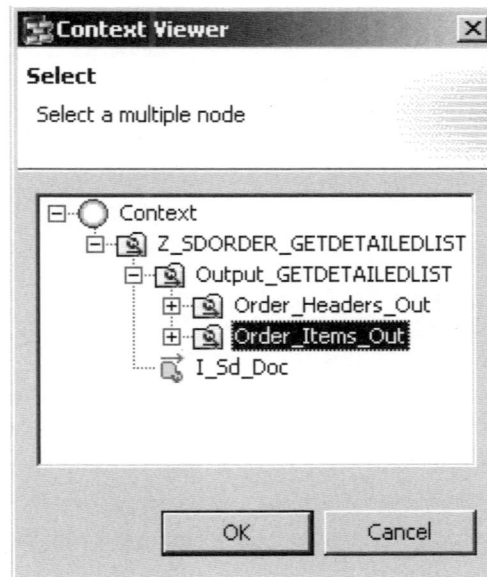

Figure 2.37   Selecting the Node Order_Item_Out

5. After assigning the data source you can define the columns to be displayed. To do that, open the context menu of the table **TableOrder_Items_Out** and select **Create Binding**. The system displays a list of all fields. Unfortunately, at this point there is no search function available, nor are the fields sorted in alphabetical order.

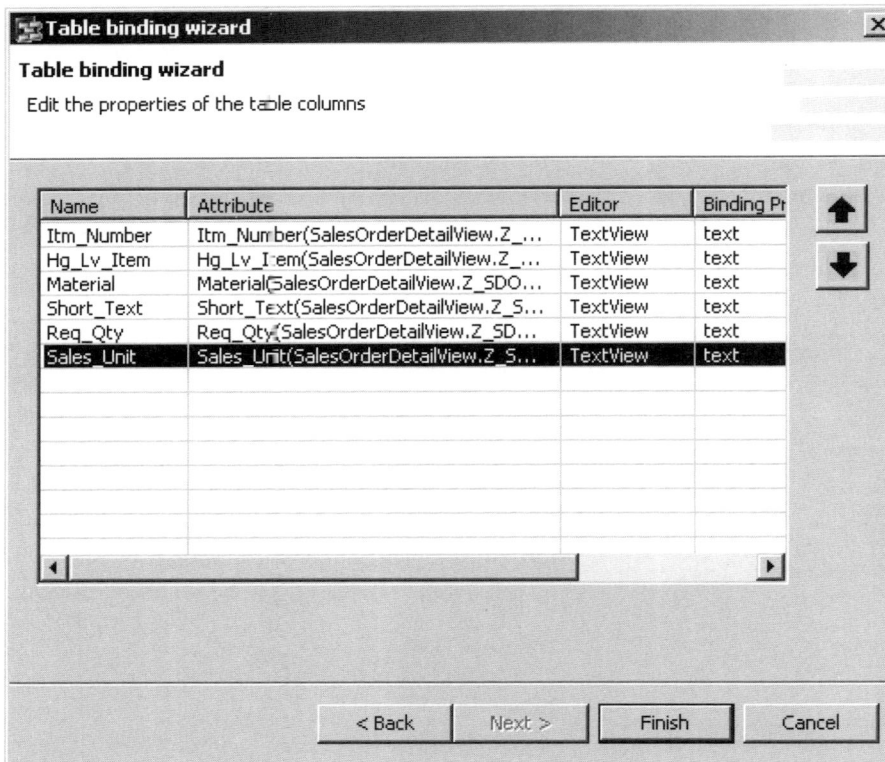

Figure 2.38 Item Data to be Displayed

6. For our display of item data, select the fields shown in Figure 2.38. Click on **Next** and sort the fields in the order you wish.

7. Click on **Finish** and save the result.

8. To place a button in our tab, which can be used to return to the results list, add a button under the **Root** element and assign the ID **BackButton** to it. Enter the description "Back to results list" in the **text** field of the **Properties**. Link the **onAction** event with the **Back** method.

Defining the Navigation

Navigation functionality between views is implemented using *inbound* and *outbound* plugs. For complete navigation, you need an inbound plug, an outbound plug, and a navigation link.

Figure 2.39 illustrates that the two views can call each other. This way we can go to the detail view and back. You can create the plugs using the graphical editor or via the context menu of a view. In the following steps we'll use the graphical editor.

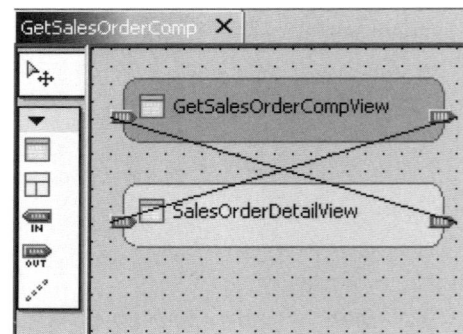

Figure 2.39 Navigation via Inbound and Outbound Plugs

1. Open the **Navigation Modeler** of the **GetSalesOrderComp** window via the context menu.

2. Click once on the pink arrow (**OUT**) in the left-hand part and then on the view **GetSalesOrderCompView**. The name of the outbound plug is ToDetailView.

3. Create another outbound plug for the view **SalesOrderDetailView** and assign the name "ToListView" to it.

4. Create two inbound plugs in the same manner by clicking on the blue arrow (**IN**). The view **GetSales-OrderCompView** contains the name "FromDetail-View", while the view **SalesOrderDetailView** shows the name "FromListView".

5. Use the navigation link to connect **ToDetailView** with **FromListView** and **ToListView** with **FromDetailView**. The Navigation Modeler should now display a screen like the one shown in Figure 2.39. You can check if your efforts were successful in Web Dynpro Explorer, as shown in Figure 2.40.

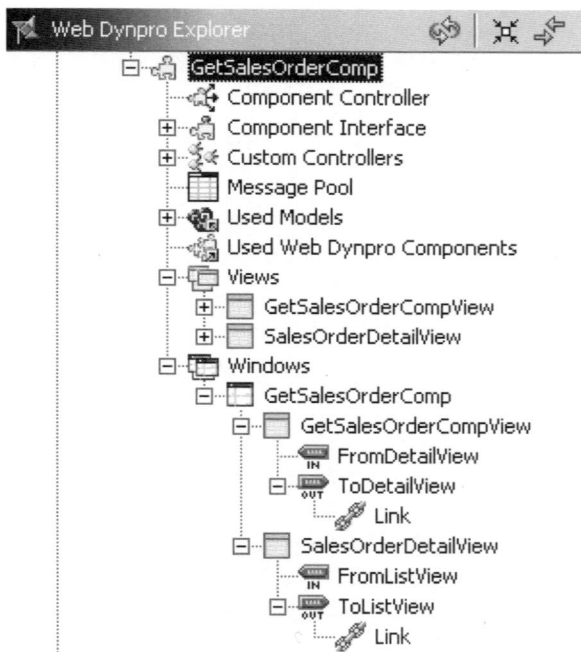

Figure 2.40 Navigation

Enhancing the UI and Context of the Order List

We must now enhance the UI of the order list so that the jump into the detail view functions properly. For this reason, we'll now link the order list with the action `GetOrderDetail` to realize the jump into the detail view.

1. Open the view **GetSalesOrderCompView** and then the **Layout** view.

2. Go to the properties of the UI element **TableSales-OrderElement**.

3. Link the event **onLeadSelect** with the action **Get-OrderDetail**.

4. Set the **selectionMode** to **single**. This way it is en-sured that only one order can be selected at this stage.

Then we must add the transfer variable `Sd_Doc_Detail` to the context of the view. That way we can ensure an easy access to the variable located in the custom control-ler.

1. Open the **Context** view in the **GetSalesOrder-CompView** view.

2. Select **New · Value Attribute** in the context menu of **Context**. Assign the name "Sd_Doc_Detail" and click on **Finish**.

3. Select **Edit Context Mapping ...** in the context menu of the new element **Sd_Doc_Detail**.

4. Select the value attribute **Sd_Doc_Detail** from the displayed context of the custom controller **GetSales-OrderCust**.

Implementation

All our preparations are complete, so that we can start the implementation. Again, you will be surprised at how little code is needed for such a complex application.

First, we'll implement the jump into the detail view: If the user is in the order list view and clicks on an order, the application is supposed to navigate to the detail view. In a previous step, we have linked the table that contains the order list with the action `onActionGetOrder-Detail`. Now we want to give life to the method.

To be able to open the required document in the detail view, we must read the requested document number in the first line of the code for the `onActionGetOrderDetail` method (see Listing 2.6), and save it temporarily in a lo-cal variable. In the next step, we'll write the document number into the context element of our custom control-ler `GetSalesOrderCust`. We assume that in the detail view the document number to be displayed is always lo-cated in the same position, which increases reusability.

Another advantage of this type of implementa-tion is that the data acquisition—that is, the model for the detail data—remains unknown at this point so that it can be replaced easily at any time. We'll use the `wdFirePlugToDetailView` method to navigate to the detail view.

```
//@@begin onActionGetOrderDetail(ServerEvent)
String i_sd_doc = wdContext.currentSales_OrdersElement().getSd_Doc();
wdContext.currentContextElement().setSd_Doc_Detail(i_sd_doc);
wdThis.wdFirePlugToDetailView();
//@@end
```

Listing 2.6   onActionGetOrderDetail Method

```
//@@begin onPlugFromListView(ServerEvent)
 String sd_doc = wdThis.wdGetGetSalesOrderCustController().wdGetContext()¬
   .currentContextElement().getSd_Doc_Detail();
  wdContext.currentZ_SDORDER_GETDETAILEDLISTElement().setI_Sd_Doc(sd_doc);
  wdThis.wdGetGetSalesOrderCustController().executeZ_SDORDER_GETDETAILEDLIST();
//@@end
```

Listing 2.7   onPlugFromListView Method

To implement these steps proceed as follows.

1. Open the view **GetSalesOrderCompView**.
2. Click on the **Implementation** tab in the detail view.
3. Find the `onActionGetOrderDetail` method and insert the code shown in Listing 2.6.
4. Save the changes.

Then we'll implement the counterpart to the jump from the order list: arrival in the detail view. In the detail view, the method `onPlugFromListView` is performed when the application comes from the order list. In the first line, we'll read the requested document number from the context of the custom controller and write it into the model in the second line. In the third line, the BAPI is called. This is done as follows:

1. Open the view **SalesOrderCompView**.
2. Click on the **Implementation** tab in the detail view.
3. Find the `onPlugFromListView` method and insert the code from Listing 2.7.
4. Save the changes.

Here is a very interesting and important point: In contrast to the view, i.e. the `GetSalesOrderCompView` view, we managed to avoid mapping the context element `Sd_Doc_Detail` in this case. We can still access that element through the relevant class hierarchy. As you can see, however, accessing it is much more complex than if we had mapped the element.

To be able to return to the order list from the detail view, we have created the `onActionBack` method in the `SalesOrderDetailView` view. Implementing the return is pretty easy, as the navigation is available as pre-defined and merely needs to be addressed. Enter the source code shown in Listing 2.8 into the `onActionBack` method.

```
//@@begin onActionBack(ServerEvent)
wdThis.wdFirePlugToListView();
//@@end
```

Listing 2.8   onActionBack Method

This completes the implementation in the views, so we can now focus on the custom controller `GetSalesOrderCust`.

The context nodes are built in the method `wdDoInit`. Because our new model Z_SDORDER_GETDETAILEDLIST also contains a new context node, we must enhance the initialization. Enhance the implementation of the `wdDoInit` method by using listings.

Finally, what's still missing is the implementation of the BAPI call Z_SDORDER_GETDETAILEDLIST in the method `executeZ_SDORDER_GETDETAILEDLIST`. Essentially, the code isn't much different from the call you have already seen in BAPI_SALESORDER_GETLIST. Thus, you can simply insert the code from Listing 2.10 into the method `executeZ_SDORDER_GETDETAILEDLIST`.

```
//@@begin wdDoInit()
// Create a new element of the context node BAPI_SALESORDER_GETLIST_INPUT
Bapi_Salesorder_Getlist_Input input = new Bapi_Salesorder_Getlist_Input();
wdContext.nodeBAPI_SALESORDER_GETLIST_INPUT().bind(input);
// Create a new element of the context node Z_SDORDER_GETDETAILEDLIST
Z_Sdorder_Getdetailedlist_Input detailedlist = new Z_Sdorder_Getdetailedlist_Input();
wdContext.nodeZ_SDORDER_GETDETAILEDLIST().bind(detailedlist);
//@@end
```

Listing 2.9 Initialization

```
//@@begin executeZ_SDORDER_GETDETAILEDLIST()
try{
// Call function module BAPI_SALESORDER_GETLIST
  wdContext.currentZ_SDORDER_GETDETAILEDLISTElement().modelObject().execute();
  }
catch (Exception ex)
  {
// If an exception occurs, output stack
  wdContext.currentContextElement().setMessage(ex.toString());
  ex.printStackTrace();
  }
//Synchronize the data in the context with the model data
wdContext.nodeOutput_GETDETAILEDLIST().invalidate();
//@@end
```

Listing 2.10 executeZ_SDORDER_GETDETAILEDLIST Method

Deploying and Running

Deploy the Web Dynpro application and run it. If a problem occurs, you should first try to rebuild the entire project. To do that, you must open the context menu of the Web Dynpro application and select **Rebuild Project**.

Especially if you work with new models or after importing or deleting a model, problems can occur that cause the application to terminate, displaying Java errors. Prior to troubleshooting the errors, you should delete the application entirely from the J2EE server, restart the server, and deploy the application again. Section 5.2 contains useful information on deleting applications.

3 Customer Portal

In Chapter 2, we developed an application for displaying sales order data. That application is supposed to be used by employees. To also provide customers with such an application in the context of an employee portal, the functionality of the application must be restricted. For our example, this means the selection must be limited to the customer numbers of the logged-on users. The data of other customers must not be displayed.

For this reason, we'll describe the necessary enhancements to the portal in Section 3.1. To avoid unintentional calls from outside, we'll cover creating a forced logon in Section 3.2. In Section 3.3, we'll show how to implement a role-based behavior in the application.

3.1 Configurations in the Portal

If a user logs on to the customer portal with a user ID, he or she most often doesn't have any relation to the internal SAP customer number. At that stage, one could be very restrictive and set a condition that specifies that there can only be one portal user per customer and the user ID be identical to the SAP customer number. However, that wouldn't be very customer-friendly. Moreover, it would mean that several users would have to use the same portal user ID, if several queries of different users of a customer are performed simultaneously.

Possible Connections

If you take a closer look at this problem, you'll soon come to the conclusion that a distinction between the SAP customer number and the portal user ID is essential. You have several options for establishing a connection between the portal user and the customer number:

▶ You could store the connection between the portal user and the SAP customer number in separate ta-

bles. The disadvantage of this would be that in addition to the user maintenance in the portal you would have to call another application for maintaining the connection between the portal user and the SAP customer number. That second application would also have to be developed in advance.

▶ Another possibility is to store all required data directly in the portal user. For this purpose, SAP Enterprise Portal enables you to use individual fields in the user administration. The benefit is that no further developments are necessary, and the data can be maintained when a new portal user is created.

Maintaining Individual Fields in User Administration

In the following steps, we'll describe the aforementioned option of maintaining individual fields in the user administration.

1. Log on as a portal administrator to SAP Enterprise Portal. In the main navigation, select **System Administration · System Configuration**.
2. Select **UM Configuration** from the detailed navigation on the left.
3. In the user administration configuration, go to the **Direct Editing** tab.
   At this point you can directly change the configuration of the user administration. But please proceed with caution, as you can change the configuration here without having the system perform any checks.
4. Find the line that contains the attribute "ume.admin. addattrs" and add the fields **Customer** and **Sales Organization** to the line, as shown in Figure 3.1. The individual fields must be separated by semicolons.
5. Remember to click on **Save all changes** after entering your changes.

Once you have entered the changes, you must restart the portal. The fields are then displayed in the user administration. To verify that, call **User Administration · Users** after the restart, select any user and go to the **Change Mode**. The newly configured fields are now displayed at the end of the account master data (see Figure 3.2).

3.2   Forcing a Logor

It hasn't been necessary so far to log on to our application. Whoever knows its URL can directly call the application through a browser. This should no longer be possible from now on, because we want to provide the sales order lists to our customers.

By performing the following steps we'll force a logon so that the application can't be used until the user has been authenticated.

1. Open the detail view of the application in SAP NetWeaver Developer Studio by double-clicking on **WDGetSalesOrder**.
2. Click on the **Application Properties** tab and then on **New**.
3. We'll use a **Pre defined** type. Use the **Browse...** button to select the application property (**sap.authentication**), and set the **value** to **true** (see Figure 3.3).
4. Click on **Finish**, save the change, and deploy the project once again. The next time you start the application, it will automatically prompt you to authenticate yourself.

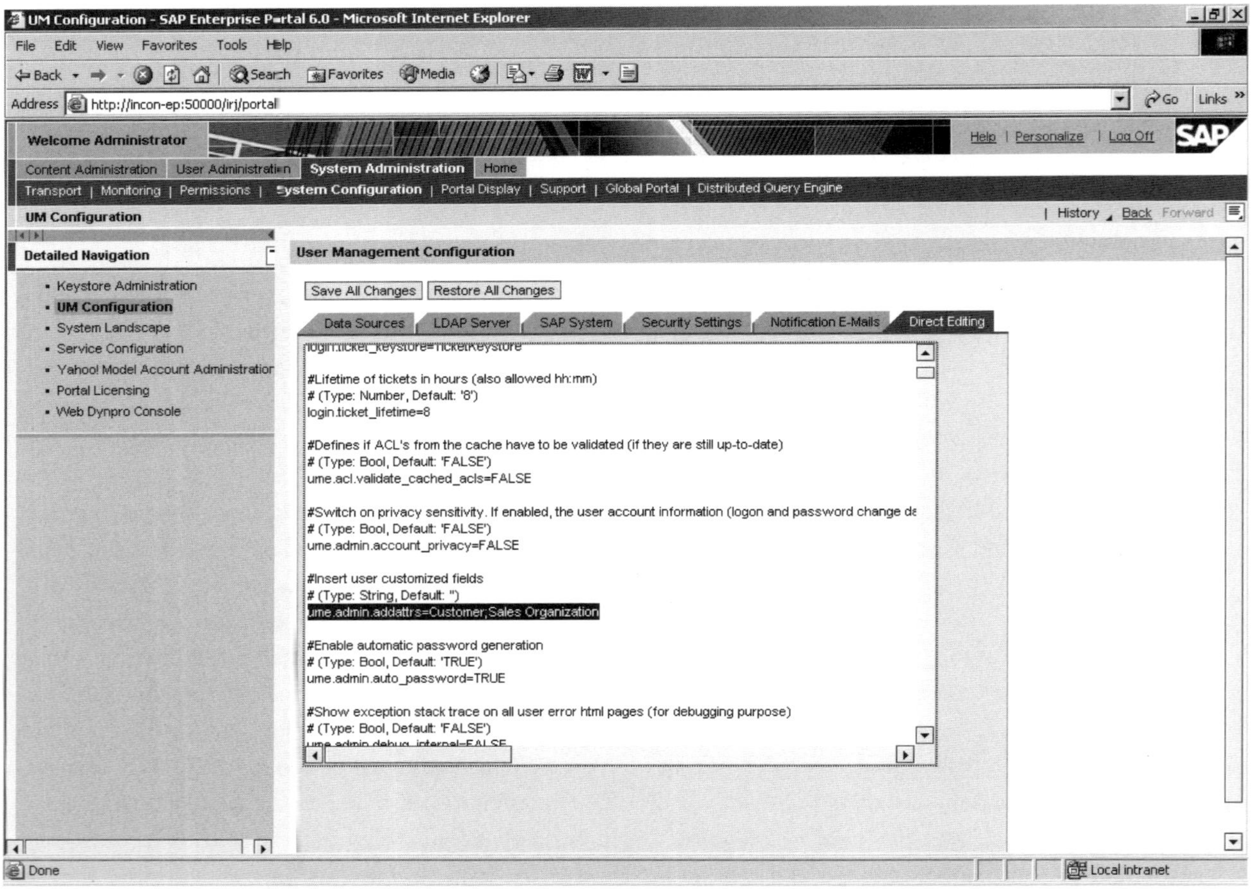

Figure 3.1   Configuring the User Administration

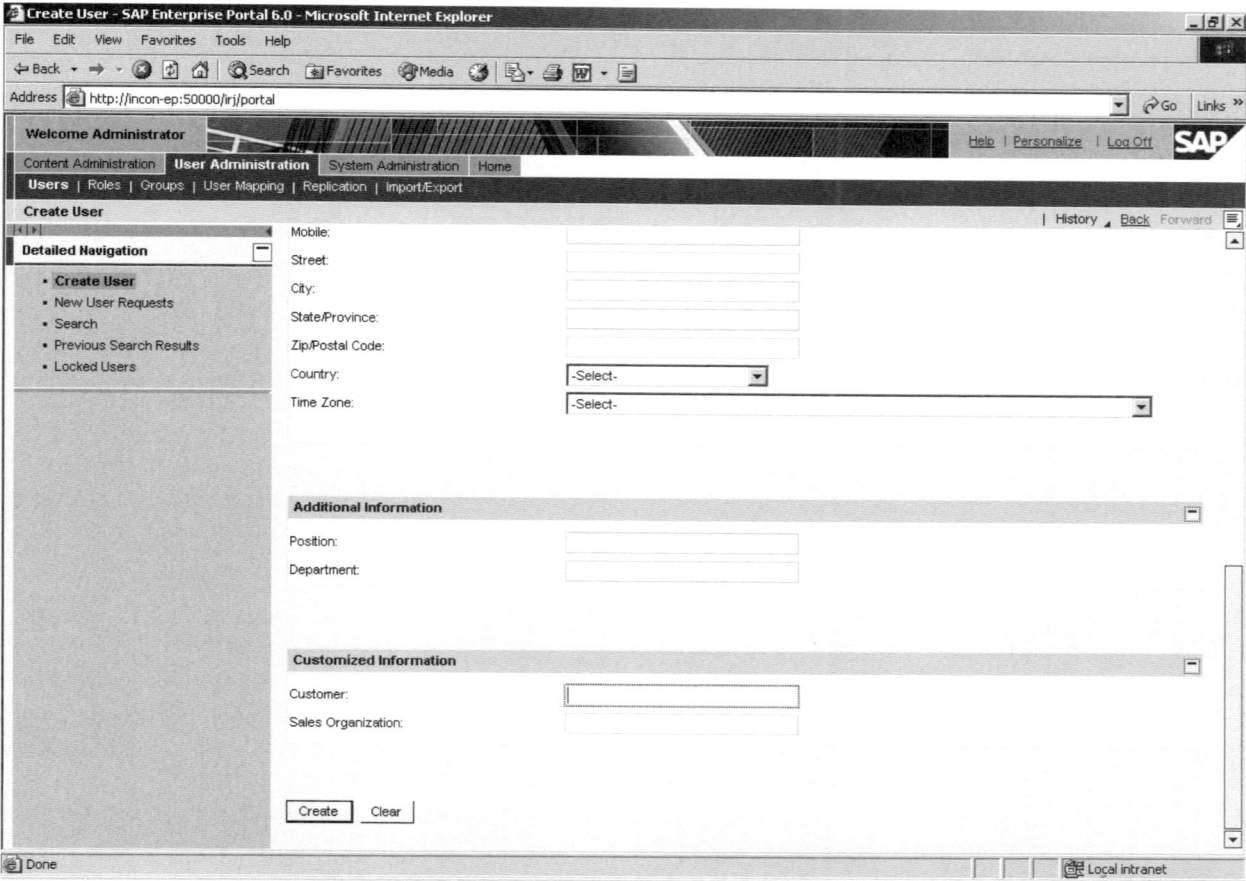

Figure 3.2 Newly Configured Fields

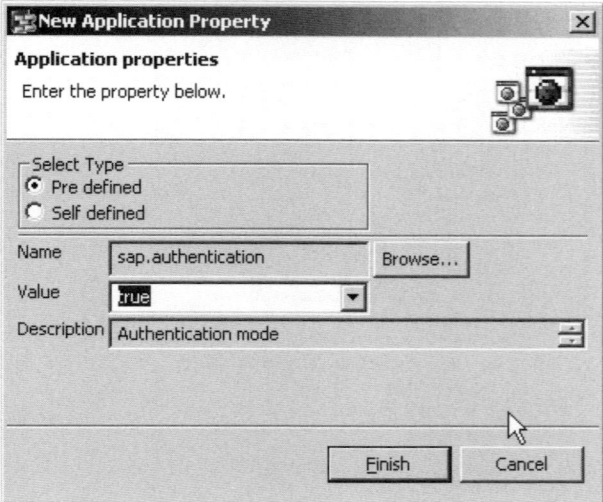

Figure 3.3 Setting the Authentication Property

3.3 Role-Based Behavior

Developing a role-based behavior is one of the technically more demanding areas in the world of Web Dynpro development. The underlying principle for role-based behavior provides for the current user to be forced to logon first via SAP Enterprise Portal. The logged-on user is then assigned roles that are checked by the application. In correspondence with the assigned roles, functions of the application then are either enhanced or restricted.

Technically speaking, this principle could be implemented in such a way that within the application the relevant roles would first be queried and the behavior would change accordingly. For our application, this would mean that we'd have to create two roles: one for the employee and one for the customer. The drawback of this direct-role query is that changes to the role concept represent entire program changes. As soon as you want to introduce a third role, such as the business partner to whom you want to assign the same rights as the customer's, you would have to customize the program.

Therefore, it makes much more sense to separate the role from the direct functionality, which can be done in SAP Enterprise Portal by using the *actions*. In our Web Dynpro application we don't ask for the role assignment but rather for the *permission* for specific actions. In the portal administration, these actions are then linked to roles. If the role concept is changed or enhanced, the actions can easily be assigned to the new roles. Figure 3.4 illustrates this concept.

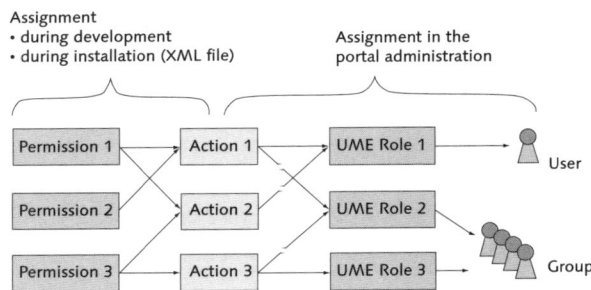

Figure 3.4 Connections Between Roles and Permissions via Actions

The implementation of role-based behavior in our application is divided into the following steps.

1. Integrating the required API
2. Creating a new package
3. Creating a new Java class
4. Creating the permission error page
5. Implementing the role-based behavior
6. Defining individual actions
7. Assigning actions to roles
8. Creating users with different roles

Integrating the required API

When you create a new Web Dynpro project, it is equipped with various predefined packages. If you want to increase the number of predefined packages, the new ones must be linked to the project. The required classes and methods are located in the package *com.sap.security.api* that contains the most important user management functions.

In the following steps we'll describe how you can bind this package to our Web Dynpro project **WDGetSalesOrder**.

1. Open the context menu of the Web Dynpro project **WDGetSalesOrder** and click on **Properties**.
2. Select **Java Build Path** and then the **Libraries** tab (see Figure 3.5).

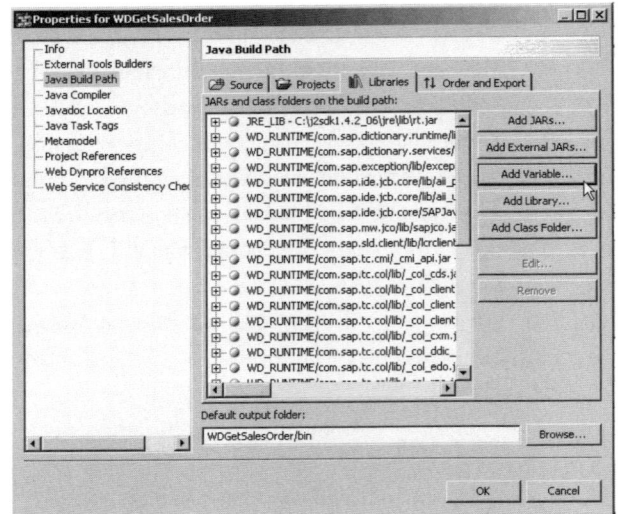

Figure 3.5 Editing the Java Build Path

3. Click on **Add Variable...**
4. Select the **ECLIPSE_HOME** variable and click on **Extend...**
5. Expand the **plugins** folder and select the JAR file **com.sap.security.api.jar**, as shown in Figure 3.6.
6. Confirm the individual dialogs with **OK**.

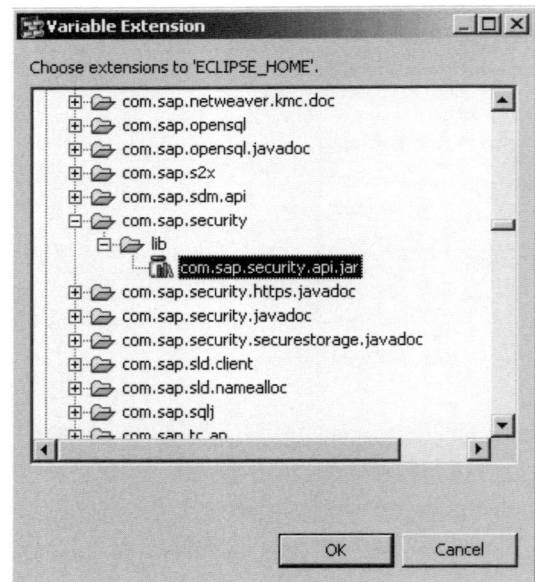

Figure 3.6 Variable Extension

Creating a New Package

We'll now create a new package in which we'll extend the *Name Permission* class of the package we just integrated. This package enables us to properly encapsulate the class extension and to reuse it in other projects, if we want to.

1. In the Web Dynpro perspective of SAP NetWeaver Developer Studio, go to the **Navigator**.
2. Open the context menu of our Web Dynpro project **WDGetSalesOrder** and click on **New · Other**.
3. Select **Java** in the dialog that opens, and then click on **Package**. Confirm this by clicking **Next**.
4. The **Source Folder** field should contain a value, as shown in Figure 3.7. The name of our new package is "com.sap.wdsecurity". Confirm this by clicking on the **Finish** button.

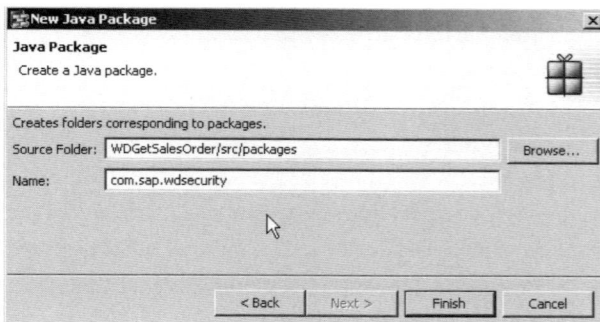

Figure 3.7 Creating a New Java Package

In the Web Dynpro perspective, the new package is now displayed below the **Navigator** tab.

Creating a New Java Class

Now that we have created a new package, we'll create a new Java class within this package.

1. Select **File · New · Other** from the main menu of SAP NetWeaver Developer Studio.
2. Select **Java** in the dialog that opens, and then click on **Class**. Confirm this dialog by clicking on the **Next** button.
3. Create the new Java class "Authorization" according to the specifications in Figure 3.8. Prior to clicking on the **Finish** button, you must select the **Superclass**. To do that, click on **Browse**.

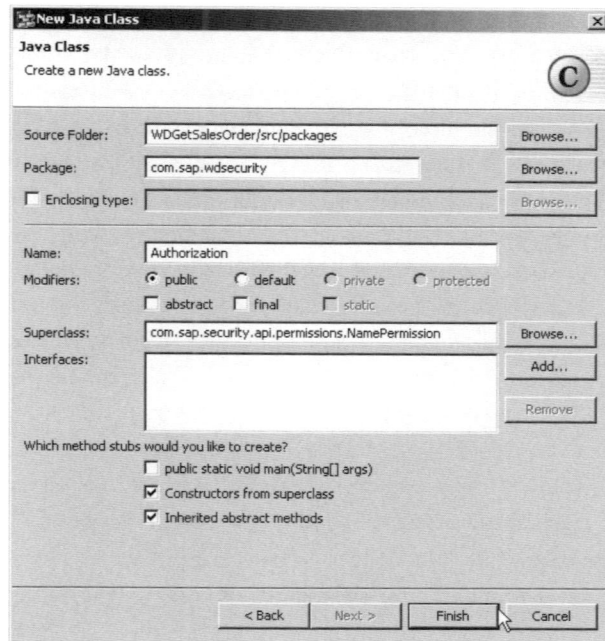

Figure 3.8 Creating the New Java Class "Authorization"

4. If you enter the first letters of the class name, you can restrict the selection of class names. Select the class name **NamePermission**, as shown in Figure 3.9, and confirm this by clicking **OK**.

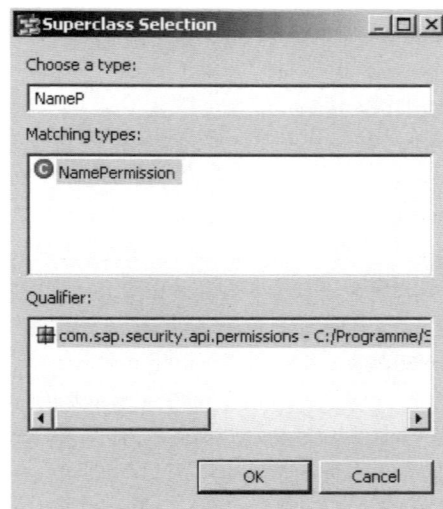

Figure 3.9 Class Selection

5. Confirm the creation of the new Java class by clicking on **Finish**.

Creating the Permission Error Page

When a user logs on to the portal, he must enter a user name and password. The portal performs an authentication check and returns an error message to the user, if the user name or password is invalid. If, however, we notice during program execution that the necessary rights for running the application haven't been assigned, i.e. if the logged-on user has been assigned neither the **employee** nor the **customer** role, we must notify the user about that and prevent him or her from further executing the application. For that notification, we'll now create the permission error page.

1. Go to SAP NetWeaver Developer Studio, open the context menu of our project and then that of the **GetSalesOrderComp** window and select **Embed View**.
2. Select **Embed new View** and click on the **Next** button.
3. Select "PermissionError" as the **View Name**. Click on **Finish**.

In the next step, we'll prepare the jump to the permission error page.

1. Go to the **Diagram View**.
2. Create an outbound plug called "ToPermissionError" in the **GetSalesOrderCompView** view.
3. Create an inbound plug called "FromGetSalesOrder-CompView" in the **PermissionError** view.
4. Link the outbound plug to the inbound plug (see Figure 3.10).
5. Save the metadata.

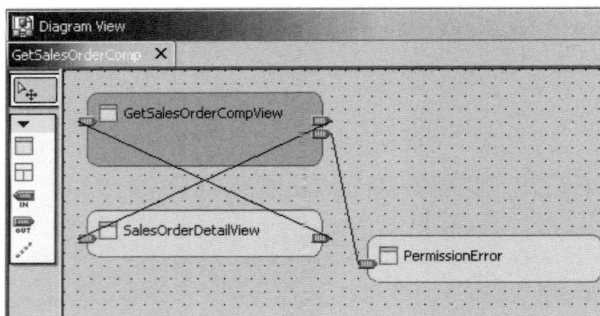

Figure 3.10 Diagram View

In the context of this example, we want to output only one message text for the user on the permission error

page. If you want to use such an application in your production system, you should apply a more sophisticated design. That is, you should at least integrate an icon in a traffic-light color and name a contact person.

1. Go to the **Layout** view of the new *PermissionError* page.
2. Open the properties of **DefaultTextView**.
3. Enter the following message in the **text** field: "You are not authorized to use the selected application."

The customer number and sales organization we prepared for read processes from the user master record—as described at the beginning of the chapter—are either released or locked, provided you are allowed to make an entry. To keep this process as simple as possible in the program we'll link the **Enabled** attributes of the two layout elements with two new context elements that must be created for this purpose. These elements can easily be modified at any time.

1. Go to the **GetSalesOrderCompView** view and click on the **Context** tab.
2. Open the context menu of the **Context** node and then select **New · Value Attribute**.
3. Enter the name "CustomerNoEnabled" and finish the creation of the new context elements by clicking on the **Finish** button.
4. Open the context menu of the new context element and select **Properties**.
5. Set the value in the **type** field to **boolean**. This enables you to set a "true" or "false" value.
6. Repeat this process and create a second element that you call "SalesOrgEnabled". Figure 3.11 displays the corresponding data.

In the next step we'll link the newly created context elements with the corresponding attributes of the layout elements.

1. Open the **Layout** view of **GetSalesOrderCompView**.
2. Set the context element **CustomerNoEnabled** in the **enabled** field in the input field properties of the customer number (**InputCustomer_Number**). To do this, you can use the search function via the button with the three dots (…).
3. Change the input field **InputSales_Organization** according to Figure 3.12.

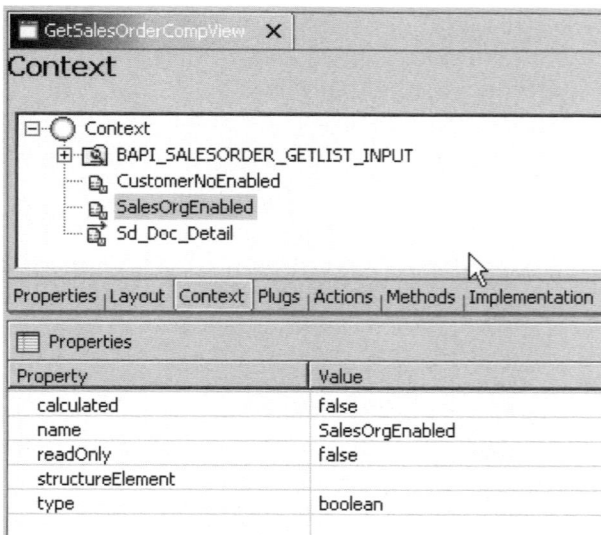

Figure 3.11 New Context Elements

Implementing the Role-Based Behavior

During the initialization of our home page, the authorization check is performed, in the `wdDoInit()` method of the `GetSalesOrderCompView` view, as shown in Listing 3.1.

The implementation begins with reading the current user. If the current user can't be identified, we jump to the error page.

Then we check the authorization for the `CALL_WDGETSALESORDER` action. We'll configure the actions later on. If the current user basically has permission to use the application, we read the stored customer number and sales organization. The read values are transferred to the relevant fields in the user interface.

If the permission for the `CUSTOMER_SELECTION_ALLOWED` action is set, the **Customer number** and **Sales organization** fields remain active, otherwise they'll be set to "disabled". This means that the user can't change the settings.

Defining Individual Actions

As described earlier, we need individual actions. The configuration of new actions is carried out via an XML file in Visual Administrator. To make things easier, we'll download an existing configuration and use it as a template for our own configuration.

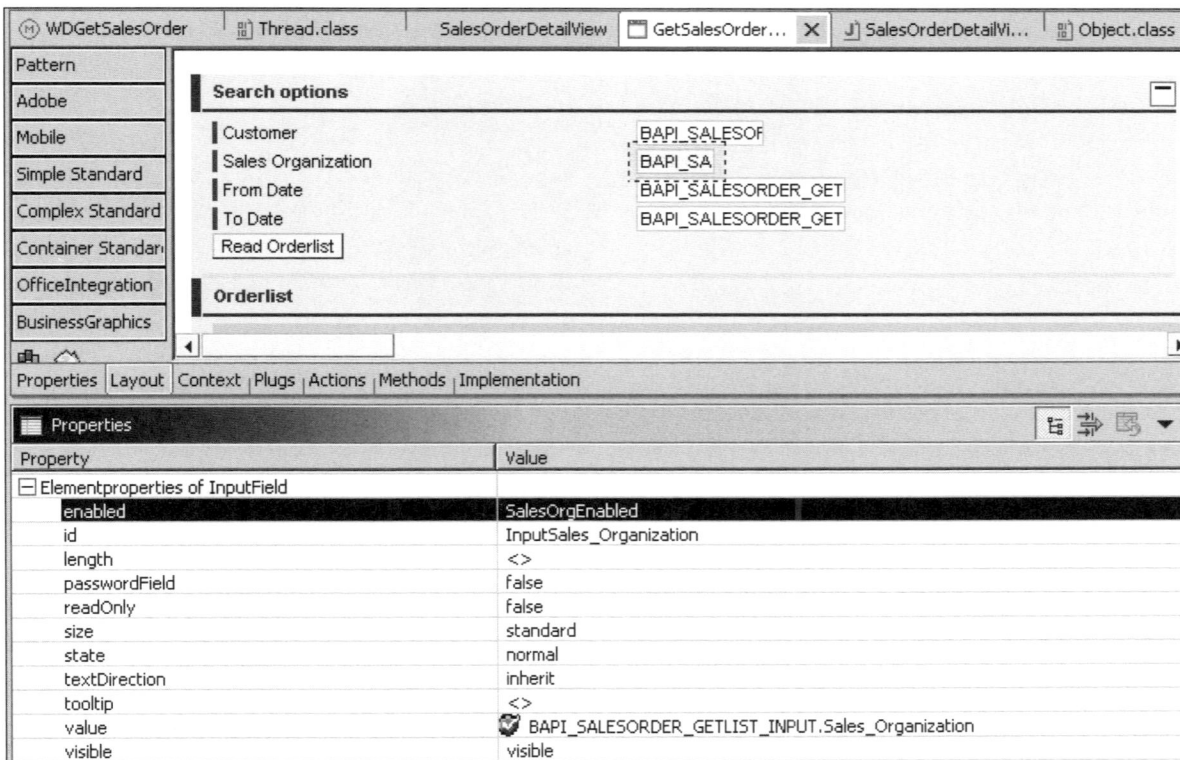

Figure 3.12 Complementing the Properties of the Sales Organization

```
public void wdDoInit()
{
  //@@begin wdDoInit()
    IWDClientUser user = null;
    IUser iuser = null;

    String kunnr = null;
    String vkorg = null;

    String[] attributeNames = null;

    try {
        user = WDClientUser.getCurrentUser();
    } catch (WDUMException e) {
        // If the current user cannot be identified:
        // Permission error
        wdThis.wdFirePlugToPermissionError();
    }

    if (user.hasPermission(new Authorization("CALL_WDGETSALESORDER"))) {
        iuser = user.getSAPUser();
        // Read all existing attributes of the user
        attributeNames =
            iuser.getAttributeNames("com.sap.security.core.usermanagement");

        // Read customer
        for (int i = 0; i < attributeNames.length; i++) {
            if (attributeNames[i].equals("Customer")) {
                kunnr =
                    iuser.getAttribute(
                        "com.sap.security.core.usermanagement",
                        "Customer")[0];
                if (kunnr != null) {
                    for (int i1 = kunnr.length(); i1 < 10; i1++) {
                        kunnr = "0" + kunnr;
                    }

                    wdContext
                        .currentBAPI_SALESORDER_GETLIST_INPUTElement()
                        .setCustomer_Number(
                        kunnr);
                }
            }
        }
```

Listing 3.1   Implementing Role-Based Behavior

```
    }

    // Read sales organization
    for (int i = 0; i < attributeNames.length; i++) {
        if (attributeNames[i].equals("Sales Organization"))
            vkorg =
                iuser.getAttribute(
                    "com.sap.security.core.usermanagement",
                    " Sales Organization")[0];
        if (vkorg != null) {
            for (int i2 = vkorg.length(); i2 < 4; i2++) {
                vkorg = "0" + vkorg;
            }
            wdContext
                .currentBAPI_SALESORDER_GETLIST_INPUTElement()
                .setSales_Organization(
                vkorg);
        }
    }

    // Open or close input fields according to authorization
    if (user
        .hasPermission(
            new Authorization("CUSTOMER_SELECTION_ALLOWED"))) {
        wdContext.currentContextElement().setCustomerNoEnabled(true);
        wdContext.currentContextElement().setSalesOrgEnabled(true);
    } else {
        wdContext.currentContextElement().setCustomerNoEnabled(false);
        wdContext.currentContextElement().setSalesOrgEnabled(false);
    }
} else {
    wdThis.wdFirePlugToPermissionError();
}

//@@end
}
```

Listing 3.1 Implementing Role-Based Behavior (cont.)

1. Start Visual Administrator via *C:\usr\sap\J2E\<System ID>\j2ee\admin\go.bat*.
2. Connect to the SAP J2EE engine via the **Default** connection. The required password is the one you entered during installation.
3. Open the **Server · Services · Configuration Adapter** node in the left-hand pane.
4. Open **cluster_data · server · persistent · com.sap.security.core.ume.service** in the right-hand pane, as shown in Figure 3.13.

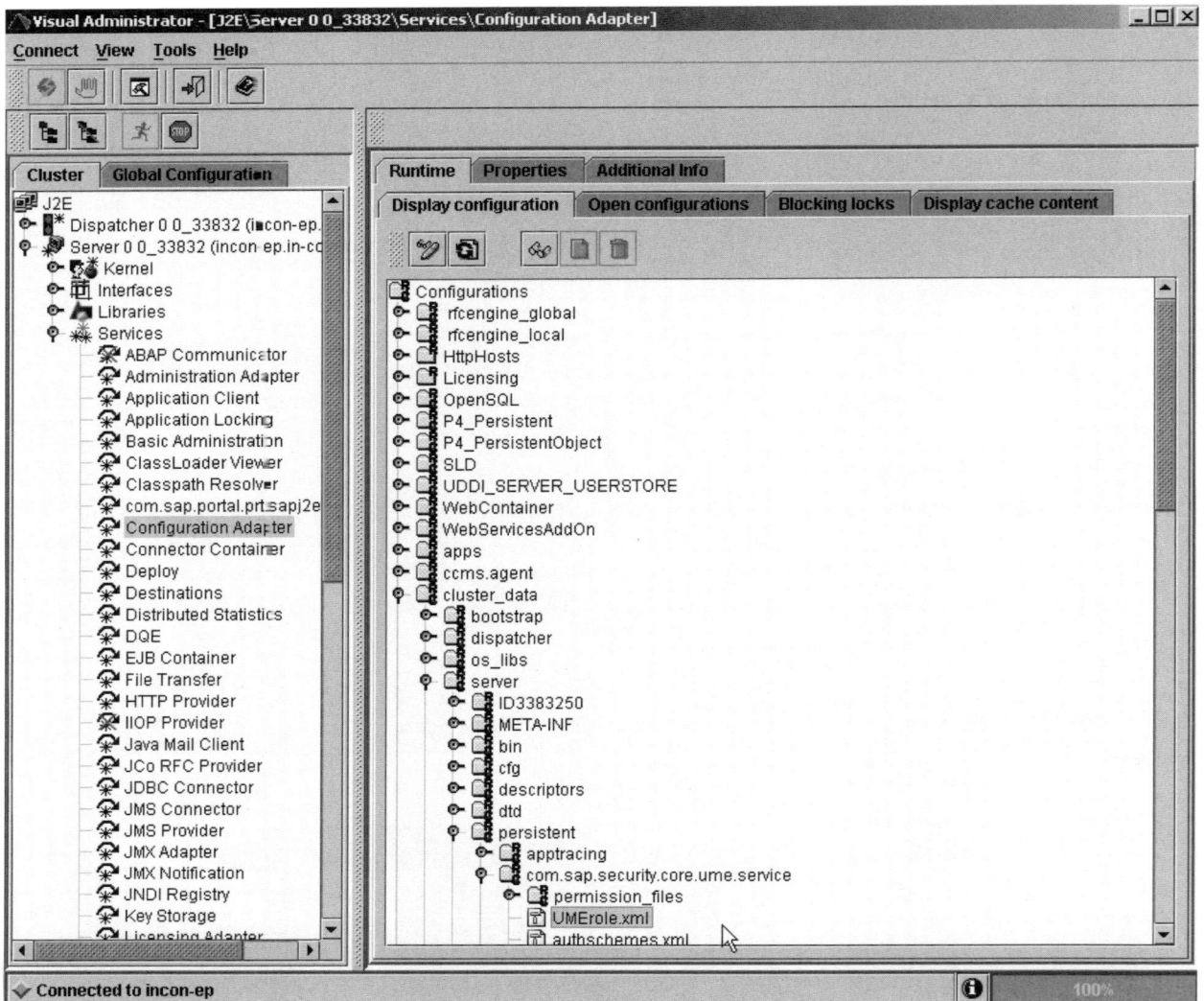

Figure 3.13   Visual Administrator

5. Open the context menu of the file **UMErole.xml** and select **Show details**.

6. Click on **Download** and save the file in a directory of your choice.

We now have a very good template for our own actions. First you should rename the file to "ZWDGSOrole.xml" in order to make sure you don't overwrite the template file. The open the file in a text editor and change its contents according to Listing 3.2.

We'll define two actions: `CallWDGetSalesOrder` and `CustomerSelectionAllowed`.

▶ `CallWDGetSalesOrder` is used to control whether a logged-on user has the permission to call our application. If the user doesn't have the permission to perform this action, the application should navigate to an error page.

▶ `CustomerSelectionAllowed` is used to control whether the user is allowed to make selections from different customers or whether a fixed customer number is displayed.

```
<!-- $Id: //shared_tc/com.sapall.security/630_REL/src/_deploy/dist/configuration/
  shared/ZWDGSOrole.xml#4 $ -->


<BUSINESSSERVICE NAME="ZWDGSO" >
  <DESCRIPTION LOCALE="en" VALUE="WD Get Sales Order"/>


  <!-- Actions -->


  <ACTION NAME="CallWDGetSalesOrder" >
    <DESCRIPTION LOCALE="en" VALUE="Permission to call WDGetSalesOrder"/>
      <PERMISSION CLASS="com.sap.wdsecurity.Authorization"
                NAME="CALL_WDGETSALESORDER" VALUE="*" />
  </ACTION>


  <ACTION NAME="CustomerSelectionAllowed" >
    <DESCRIPTION LOCALE="en" VALUE="Permission to select different Customer No"/>
      <PERMISSION CLASS="com.sap.wdsecurity.Authorization"
       NAME="CUSTOMER_SELECTION_ALLOWED" VALUE="*" />
  </ACTION>


</BUSINESSSERVICE>
```

Listing 3.2 XML File for New Actions

After saving the file, you can include it into the configuration in the next step:

1. Start the Visual Administrator.
2. Open the nodes **cluster_data · server · persistent · com.sap.security.core.ume.service**, as described earlier, and then open the context menu.
3. Select **Create sub-node**.
4. In the dialog that opens, select **File-entry** and click on **Upload**. Select the file we just created (*ZWDGSOrole.xml*) and click on **Open**. Click on **Create** and close the window (see Figure 3.14).
5. Close Visual Administrator and restart the SAP J2EE engine.

Assigning Actions to the Roles

In the last step, we must assign the actions we just created to the individual roles we already created in Chapter 2: **Customer** and **Employee**.

1. Start the user administration via *http:// <YourPortalserver>:<Portnumber>/useradmin* and logon as a user who owns administrator rights.

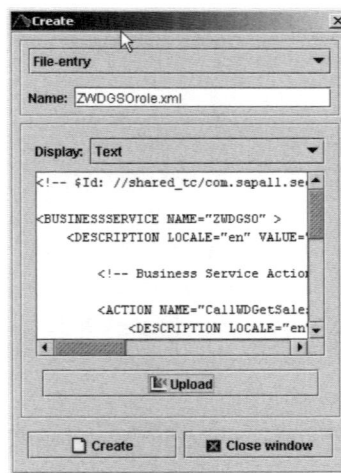

Figure 3.14 Uploading New Actions

2. Select **Roles** in the left-hand pane.
3. Find the **Employee** role, select it and click on the **Change/Display** button.
4. Assign the actions **ZWDGSO.CallWDGetSalesOrder** and **ZWDGSO.CustomerSelectionAllowed** to the **Employee** role, as shown in Figure 3.15.

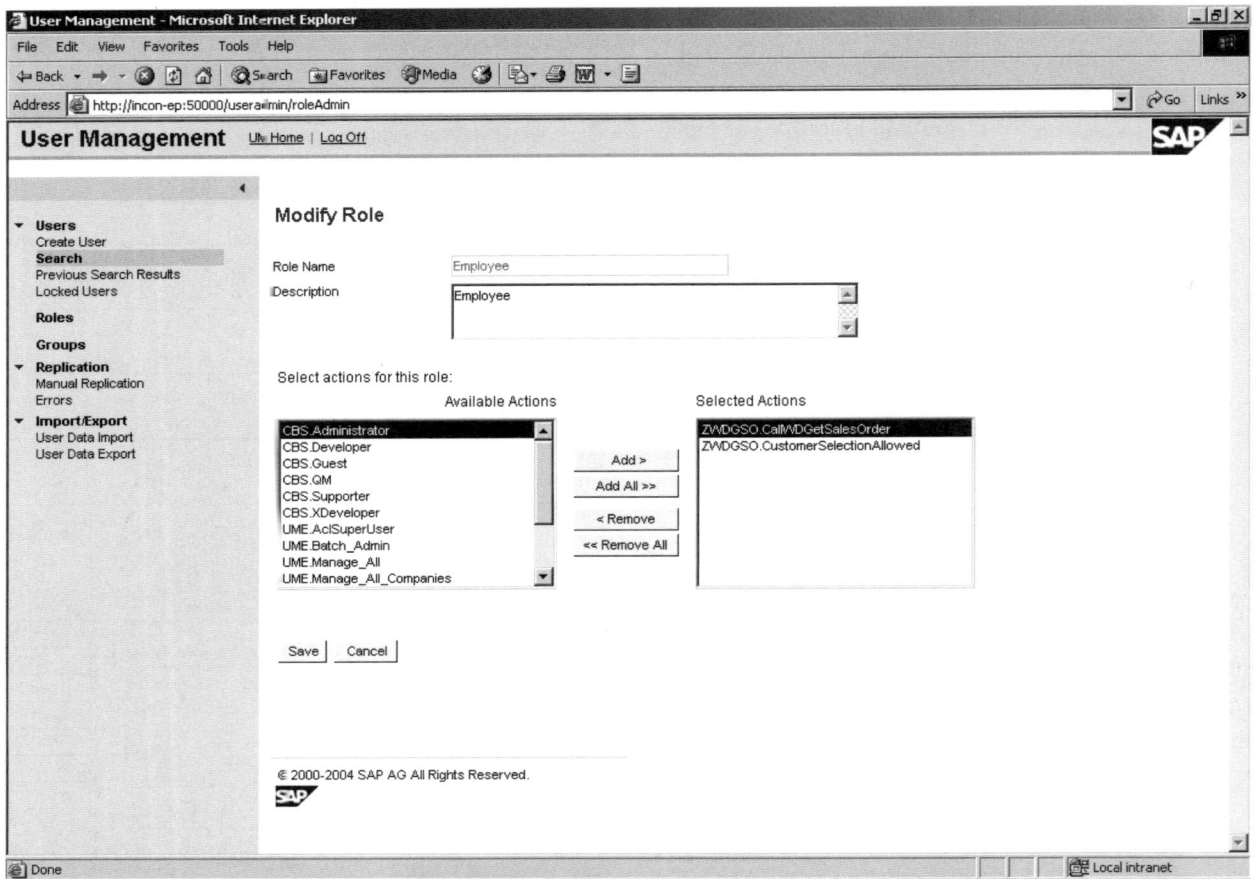

Figure 3.15   Assigning Actions to a Role

5. Save the changed role.
6. Assign the **ZWDGSO.CallWDGetSalesOrder** action to the **Customer** role. This role is not assigned the **ZWDGSO.CustomerSelectionAllowed** action. After all, we don't want to allow the customer to browser through all the customer numbers.

Creating Users with Different Roles

After creating a user with the **Employee** role and one with the **Customer** role you can verify the result. In Figure 3.16, the user was assigned the **Customer** role, which means that the **Customer number** and **Sales organization** fields are disabled.

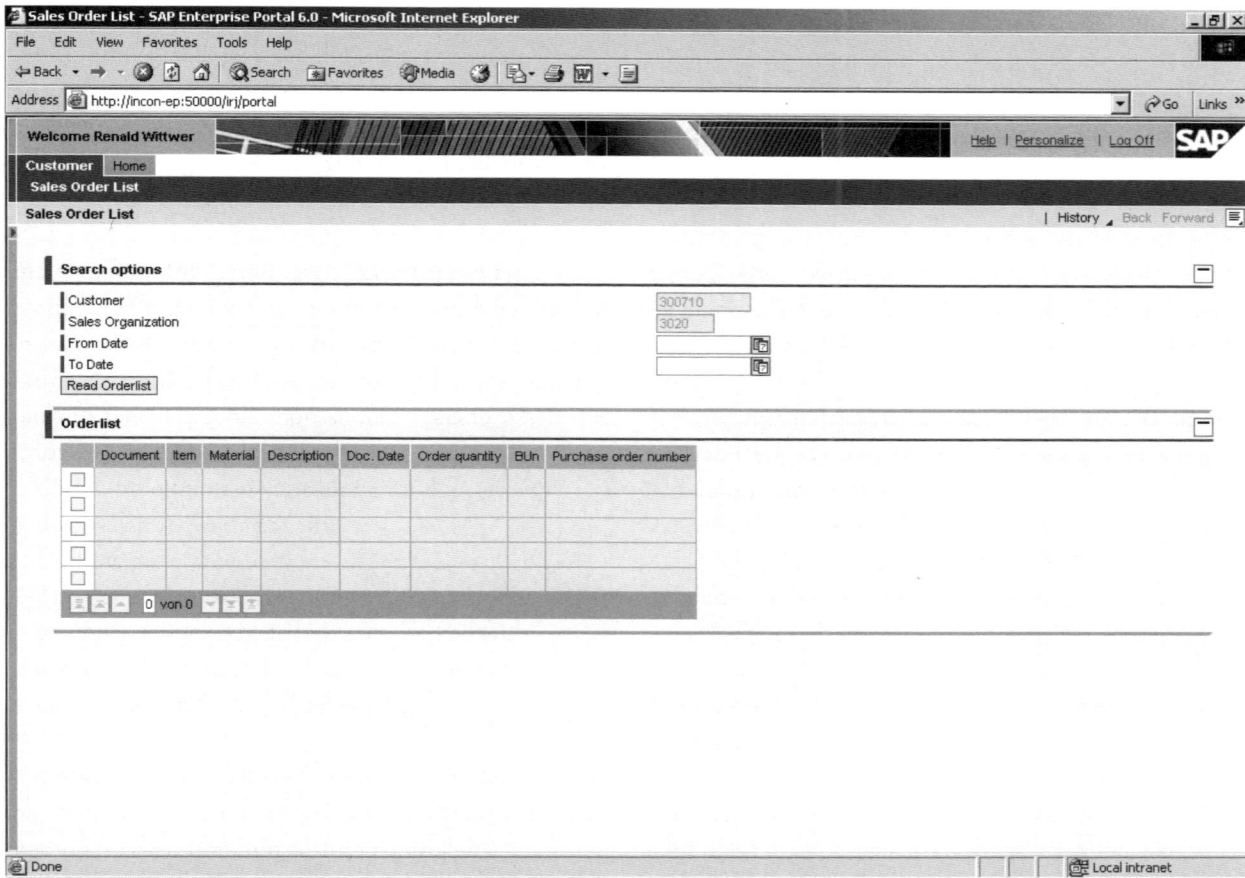

Figure 3.16 Sales Orders List for Customers

4 Partner Portal

In this chapter, we'll show how to develop a portal application that can be used to the same extent by employees and customers and by suppliers. The employee data from the HR module (personnel management) will be used to provide a phone list via the portal for everyone who's interested.

Section 4.1 contains general considerations, and in this context we'll compare BSPs with Web Dynpro. Then, we'll implement the phone list (Section 4.2), take a look at the topic of authentication in a BSP application (Section 4.3), and finally integrate our application in the portal (Section 4.4).

4.1 Phone List

Prior to making such an application available to the outside world, you should consider the consequences this step entails. With a bit of skill, for instance, one could query the number and names of all employees, which means your company would become transparent. Moreover, the phone extensions of all employees could be queried so that even upper management could be called directly.

If you are aware of these implications and still wish to proceed, you can make the application accessible for your partners. Otherwise, the phone list at least is of considerable use internally.

Business Server Pages

In addition to the techniques demonstrated so far, we'll develop the phone list using *Business Server Pages* (BSPs).

The fact that BSPs are developed in ABAP certainly speaks well for them. In many IT departments of companies that run SAP production systems, the Java know-how is close to non-existent, whereas most of the IT peo-ple are familiar with ABAP. For an ABAP expert, it's easy to understand BSPs.

Another benefit of a BSP is that it is independent of UI elements. It can use predefined extensions such as *HTML Business* (HTMLB) so that the user interface looks exactly like a Web Dynpro interface. Moreover, you can also use customized UI elements, extensions, or direct HTML in BSP applications. This is particularly important if you must comply with corporate-identity guidelines that exceed the customizing capacity of a Web Dynpro UI.

In contrast to the Web Dynpro technology, in BSPs the UI is not saved in a descriptive form, but rather directly in HTML or HTMLB. Although this means that you only can access the application through a Web browser, it enables you to use JavaScript and other browser-based technologies such as applets. This can be a big advantage, especially if you want to execute certain checks on the client in order to reduce the number of server requests.

This aspect represents another disadvantage of Web Dynpro because it provides no way of influencing the point in time at which a server request is performed. Some Web Dynpro UI elements automatically run a server request when you click on them, which can drastically affect the system performance, especially if the Internet connection is slow.

Another argument in favor of using BSPs is that you can develop *stateless* applications. This means that the server processes the request and deletes the transaction, which reduces the load if many users are logged on at the same time. The drawback is that the developer himself must take care of restoring the environment information. However, SAP provides some good tools for that task. You can also develop a *stateful* BSP application. Web Dynpro applications are always stateful.

For our phone list we want to make sure it can be operated intuitively. As shown in Figure 4.1, we want to display the selection criteria in the upper area, and the results list in the lower part. The application consists of this one screen only.

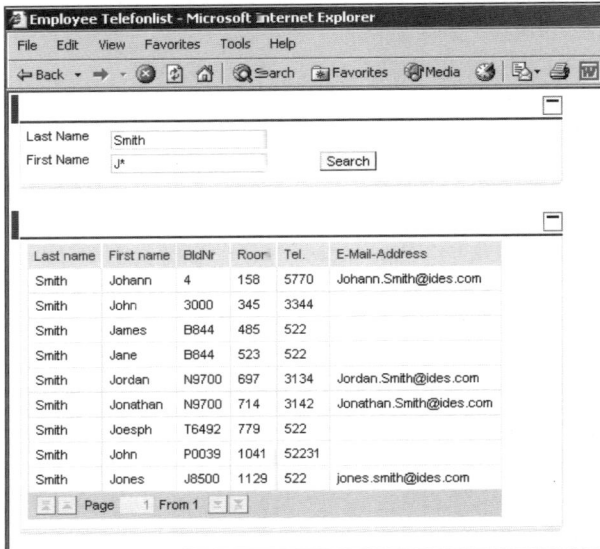

Figure 4.1   Structure of the Application

Creating a Package

We can assign the entire development of the phone list application to one package. The package concept is an enhancement of the development-class concept. Packages are used for the technical disintegration, encapsulation, and decoupling of an SAP system.

BSP applications are developed using SAP GUI. All the steps listed in the following sections are performed in SAP GUI, unless otherwise stated.

1. Go to Transaction SE80. To do that, you can either enter the transaction code into the command field or navigate through the following menu path: **SAP Menu · Tools · ABAP Workbench · Overview · Object Navigator**.

2. Select the **Package** entry in the selection box displayed.

3. Specify a package name that corresponds to your company's naming conventions. In our example we'll call the package "Z_PORTAL" as we'll collect all future developments of portal applications in this package. If you anticipate a large number of such applications, a more detailed structure may be useful.

4. The system notifies you that the package doesn't exist and will now be created; answer **Yes**.

5. In the next step the system requires further details about the package. Complete the fields, as shown in Figure 4.2, and confirm the dialog by clicking on the **Save** button in the lower left-hand corner.

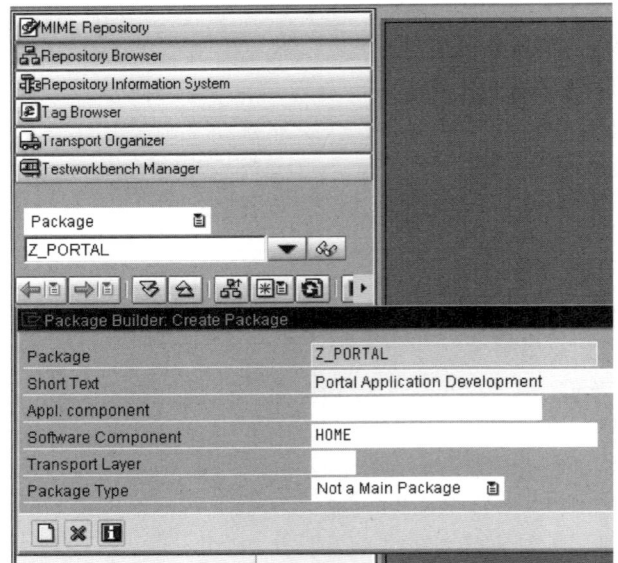

Figure 4.2   Creating a New Package

6. The system may now prompt you for a transport request. Create a new transport request.

The creation of the Z_PORTAL package has now completed and the package can be used for future developments.

Creating a BSP Application

A BSP application is a functionally complete application and can be compared to a transaction in the classical R/3 system. In terms of technology, however, it differs from an R/3 transaction even though both of them have been developed in the ABAP programming language. In addition to many other differences, a BSP application is addressed via a browser (or another mobile device), and not through SAP GUI. Unlike an R/3 transaction, a BSP application can be developed as stateless. Furthermore, the programming model of a BSP application is similar to that of other server pages environments (Java Server Pages/JSP, Active Server Pages/ASP).

Within a BSP application, the HTML pages contain the actual application and presentation logic. Note that a good BSP developer should separate the business logic as much as possible from the application.

So let's begin with creating a new BSP application.

1. Go to Transaction SE80.
2. Select **Repository Browser** on the left, and **BSP Application** in the Object Navigator.
3. Enter the name of the application, in this case that's "Z_EMP_COMM", which stands for *Employee Communication*, and confirm your entries.
4. The system displays the **Create BSP Application** dialog, and the name of the BSP application is pre-set. Enter a descriptive text as a short description, for instance "Phone list". Confirm the dialog.
5. In the next step, you must assign the new BSP application to a package. To do that, we'll use the **Z_POR-TAL** package we just created.
6. Confirm the transport request suggested by the system. This should be the transport request that already contains the package.

The BSP application has now been successfully created.

Creating a BSP Page

In the next step, we'll create a BSP page that consists of several components. The user interface is described in the **Layout**. Several event handlers are available that are called at defined points in time. Two important event handlers are `OnInitialization` and `OnInputProcessing`: `OnInitialization` is mainly used for acquiring data, while the `OnInputProcessing` event handler processes user entries. We'll describe these event handlers in more detail later.

In the page attributes, you can define variables that are displayed in the layout as well as in the event handlers.

If a BSP application is called via a corresponding URL and no HTML page opens, the SAP Web AS calls the *default.htm* page. This page can be compared to the *index. htm* page of other Web servers. Since our application won't contain more than one page, we'll simply call the page *default.htm*.

1. You're still in the Object Navigator (Transaction SE80) and within the BSP application **Z_EMP_COMM** you just created.

2. Open the context menu of the **Z_EMP_COMM** object and select **Create · Page**.
3. Enter the **Name** and **Description** for the new page in the dialog that opens: The name is "default.htm", and as a description you can enter the text "employee phone list". Accept the suggested page type, **Page with Flow Logic**. Confirm the page.
4. The *default.htm* page has been created with the standard layout. Save and activate both the BSP application and the new page.
5. Figure 4.3 displays the structure of the new BSP application, and Figure 4.4 shows the predefined standard layout of the new *default.htm* page.

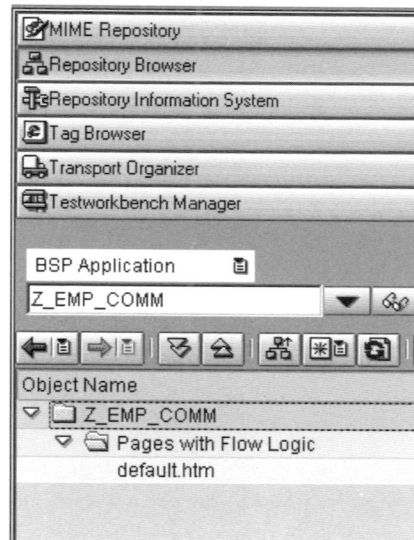

Figure 4.3 New BSP Application

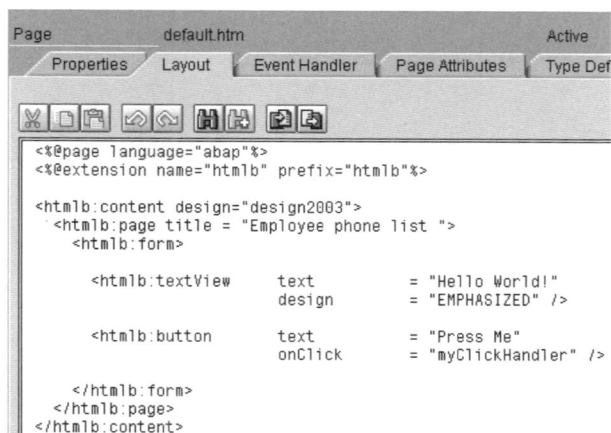

Figure 4.4 Standard Layout

Creating an Application Class

For each application, you can store an application class in which the business logic of the application is implemented. If no application class is stored, the developer is automatically provided with the methods of the CL_BSP_ APPLICATION class. The use of an application class enables the separation of user interface and business logic. This enables you to re-use the business logic in other applications.

To be able to use the methods of the basic class CL_ BSP_APPLICATION we'll simply derive our application class from that basic class.

1. Go to Transaction SE24 (Class Builder) either by entering the transaction code into the command field or via the following menu path: **SAP Menu · Tools · ABAP Workbench · Development · Class Builder**.
2. The name of the new class is "Z_CL_BSP_EMP_ COMM". Click on **Create**.
3. Then the system prompts you to select the object type. Keep the suggested setting **Class**, and confirm this.
4. In the following step, you can store additional data for the class. Enter the text "Application class for BSP Z_EMP_COMM" in the **Description** field. You can accept all other fields (see Figure 4.5). Save the new class.

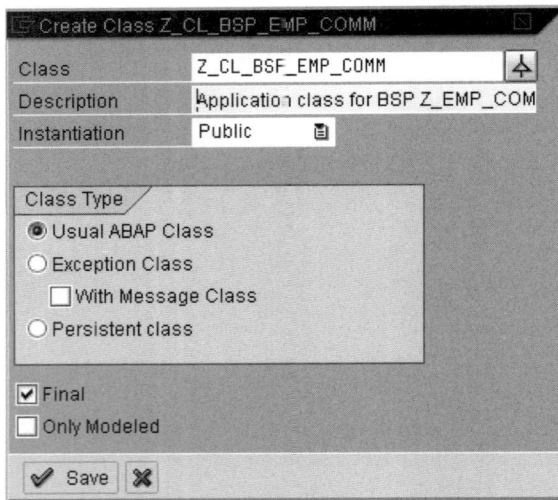

Figure 4.5 Creating a Class

5. Assign the new class to our **Z_PORTAL** package and select an appropriate transport request.

You are now in the *Class Builder,* where you can edit the newly created class by using the various tabs provided. Before we can begin implementing the new methods, we want to assign the superclass CL_BSP_APPLICATION to our new class.

1. Go to the **Properties** tab.
2. Click on **Superclass**. The field **Superclass** opens.
3. Enter CL_BSP_APPLICATION into this field.
4. Activate the new class via **Class · Activate** or by clicking on the relevant button in the menu bar.

Maintaining the Application Class in the BSP Application

Having created the application class, we must now assign it to our BSP application.

1. Start Transaction SE80 and open the BSP application **Z_EMP_COMM**.
2. Open the detail view of the BSP application by double-clicking on the **Z_EMP_COMM** object.
3. Go to the **Properties** tab.
4. Activate the **Change Mode** (**Ctrl + F1**).
5. Maintain the application class you just created in the corresponding field (see Figure 4.6). Save the BSP application and activate it.

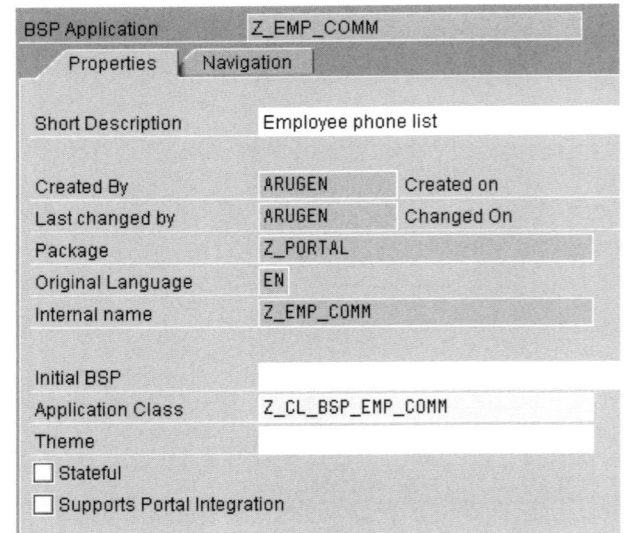

Figure 4.6 Custom Application Class

Creating a Customizing Table

Although the application we are developing is rather small, it does make sense to store specific information in a table that can be maintained.

We'll store the RFC target system for the BAPIs to be called in a separate Customizing table. That's necessary because our application will run in different environments (development, test, and production environments) and it may be the case that the data is retrieved from different systems. In a best-case scenario we won't need any additional system for the data retrieval. However, in order to ensure a proper decoupling of the presentation logic and the business logic, we should have a variable data-retrieval system.

In the Java area, you can use the functions of the *System Landscape Directory* (SLD). The ABAP world doesn't provide anything similar to that, but we can simply construct something.

1. Go to Transaction SE11 (Dictionary), either by entering the transaction code into the command field or via the following menu path: **SAP Menu · Tools · ABAP Workbench · Development · ABAP Dictionary**.

2. Check the radio button **Database table** and enter the name of the new database table, "ZBSP_RFCDEST". Click on **Create**.

3. You are now in the **Delivery and Maintenance** tab of the table maintenance. Enter the required data, as shown in Figure 4.7.

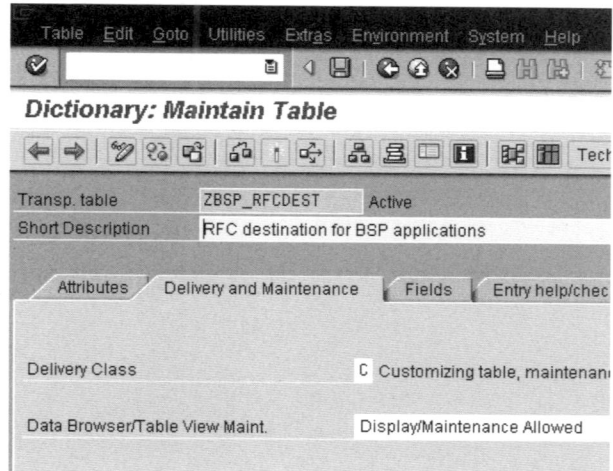

Figure 4.7 Delivery and Maintenance of our Customizing Table

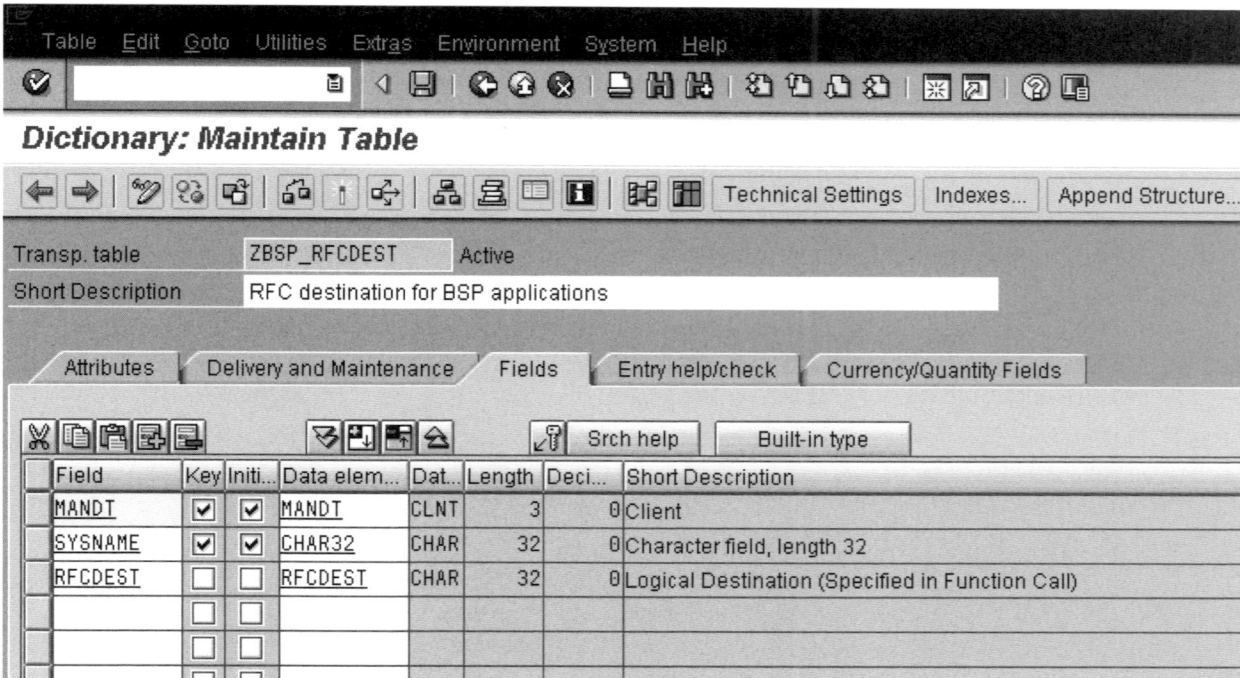

Figure 4.8 Maintaining the Table

4. Go to the **Fields** tab and maintain the fields according to Figure 4.8. Select the **Client** and **SysName** fields as key fields. We use the **SysName** field to identify the system, and in the **RFCDest** field we can maintain the actual RFC destination.

5. After maintaining the fields, you must save the table structure. During the saving process, the system prompts you for the package. Use **Z_PORTAL** again.

6. Select **Goto · Technical Settings**. Select **Organization and Customizing** in the **Data class** field, and choose the smallest option provided for the size category.

7. Activate the buffering and select **Fully Buffered** as the buffering type. Save your entries and return to the table overview.

8. Activate the new table via **Table · Activate** or by clicking on the corresponding button in the menu bar

At this point, we have created a new table, and we now want to maintain the relevant data for our application. It is quite useful to generate a maintenance interface for customizing tables using the table-maintenance generator. When doing this, note that we don't need any recording for this table. We don't want to transport the customizing of this table, but rather to maintain it individually in each system. At this point, however, we'll take a shortcut.

1. Select **Utilities · Table Contents · Create Entries**. In our system environment we don't want to call the function module on a remote system, but on the same system, that's why the RFC destination is "NONE".

2. The system to be called is assigned the name "R3HR" as the read data originates from the HR module. Save your entry as shown in Figure 4.9.

3. Save the new entry by clicking on the corresponding icon in the menu bar.

Creating a Data-Transfer Structure

The BAPIs used usually provide the requested data in a form that can't be used immediately. The required data is distributed across several internal tables and must first be mapped, but it often happens that the amount of data provided is much bigger than what is actually needed. To establish a lean communication between the systems you can create *data transfer structures*.

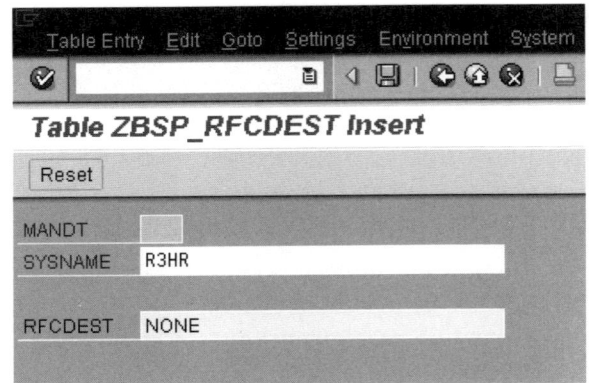

Figure 4.9   Adding a Data Record to Table ZBSP_RFCDEST

For reading data, we'll use the BAPI BAPI_EMPLOYEE_ GETDATA in which five results lists are provided that contain the data we need. For this reason, we'll create a data transfer structure:

1. Start Transaction SE11 in SAP GUI.

2. Select **Data type** and enter the name of the new structure, "ZEMP_COMMLIST". Click on **Create**.

3. The type can be further specified in the dialog that opens. Select the **Structure** entry and confirm the selection.

4. Enter the data for the new structure, as shown in Figure 4.10.

5. Save and activate the new structure and assign it to the **Z_PORTAL** package.

Now we need a table type of the structure we just created so that we can immediately create an internal table. A table type describes the structure and functional properties of an internal table in an ABAP program.

1. Call Transaction SE11 once again.

2. Select **Data type** and enter the name "ZEMP_COMMLIST_T". It is a commonly used method to add the letter "T" to the name of a table type for a structure. Click on **Create**.

3. Select **Table type** and confirm the pop-up window.

4. Maintain the **Short text** field. The row structure of the table type can be defined in the **Line type** field. Enter the structure "ZEMP_COMMLIST" here (see Figure 4.11).

5. Save the new table type, assign it to the **Z_PORTAL** package and activate it.

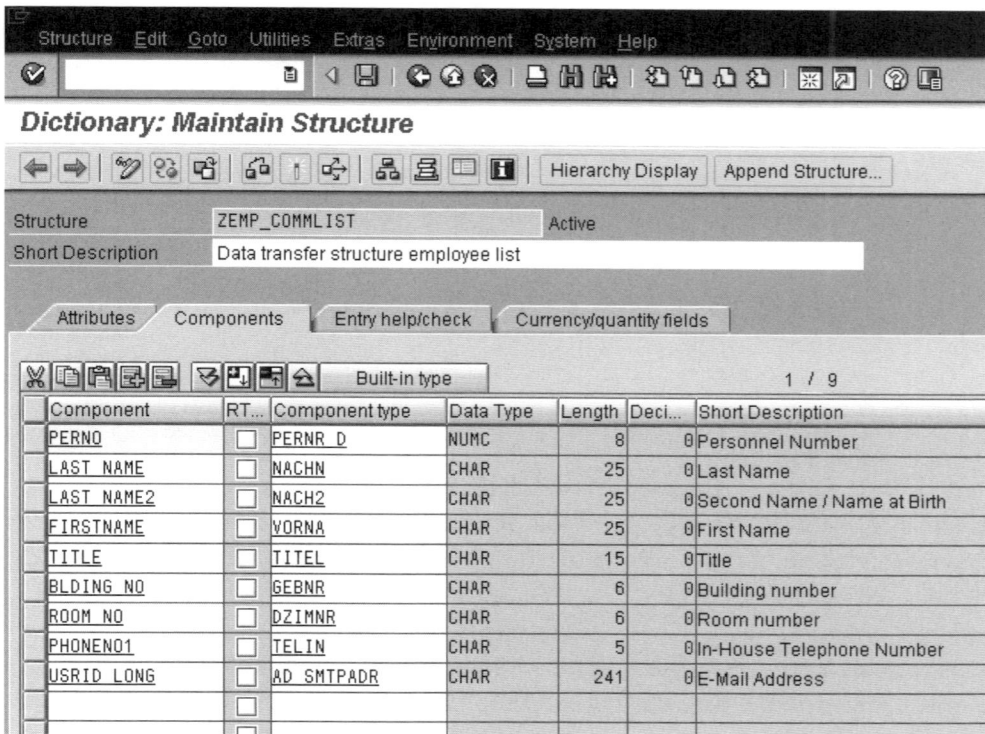

Figure 4.10 Data Transfer Structure "Employee List"

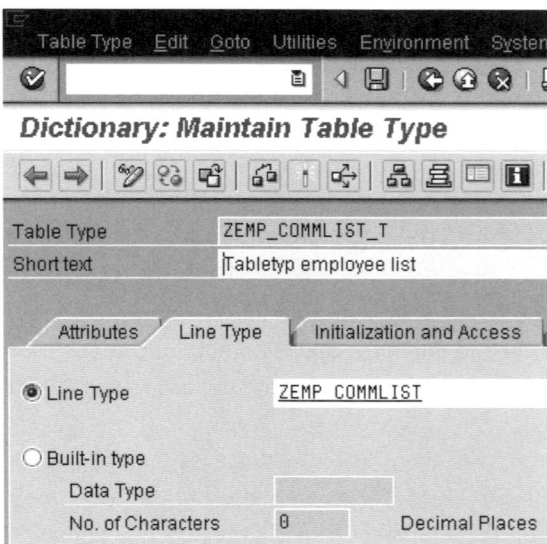

Figure 4.11 Table Type for Employee List

4.2 Implementing the Phone List

A BSP page consists of different events and the layout. In either of these areas you can define variables that can't be accessed from outside the event. Cross-event and cross-layout variables must be created in the page attributes.

Page Attributes

For our application, we first of all need the employee list which is an internal table called "COMMLIST_T". The type of this internal table is "ZEMP_COMMLIST_T".

Moreover, we'll use the variables LASTNAME and FSTNAME for transferring the input values. To be able to fill these variables from outside we must check the **Auto** column. We'll get back to this with a description later.

1. Go into the Object Navigator (Transaction SE80).
2. Open our BSP application **Z_EMP_COMM** and then the BSP page **default.htm**.
3. Go to the **Page Attributes** tab.
4. Maintain these page attributes as shown in Figure 4.12.

Layout

In the next step, we'll create the layout for the page. With BSPs you can either define the HTML code by yourself or use predefined elements.

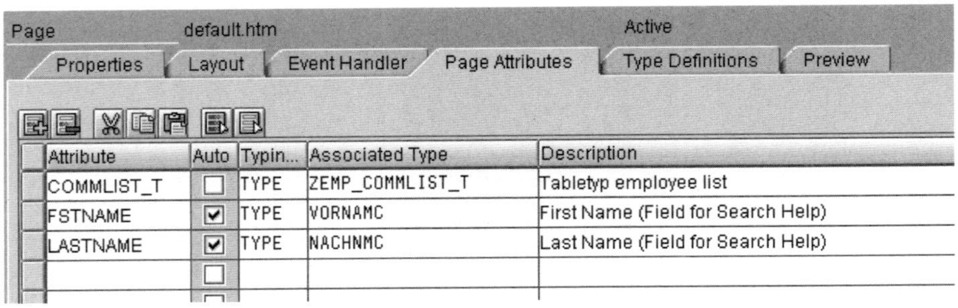

Attribute	Auto	Typin...	Associated Type	Description
COMMLIST_T	☐	TYPE	ZEMP_COMMLIST_T	Tabletyp employee list
FSTNAME	☑	TYPE	VORNAMC	First Name (Field for Search Help)
LASTNAME	☑	TYPE	NACHNMC	Last Name (Field for Search Help)
	☐			

Figure 4.12 Page Attributes

BSP Extensions are HTMLB elements[1] provided by SAP that have the advantage of enabling you to quickly develop a well-designed uniform user interface. We don't need to take care of the details of individual elements and then test our own implementation on various browsers. Instead, we'll describe the user interface using HTMLB elements very similar to HTML.

The layout of a BSP application that has been developed with HTMLB elements and runs in SAP Enterprise Portal can't be differentiated from a Web Dynpro application. As a matter of fact, the Web Dynpro and HTMLB elements have the same origin.

In the following steps, we'll develop the layout using HTMLB elements.

1. Start the Object Navigator (Transaction SE80) and open our BSP application **Z_EMP_COMM**.
2. Open the **default.htm** page and go to the **Layout** tab.

This "fresh" BSP page described here is structured as shown in Listing 4.1. The system presents a small "Hello World" application that contains an input button. In this predefined page you can already clearly see the structure of an HTMLB page.

The page starts with the tag `<%@page language="abap"%>`, which means that the inserted server-side code is ABAP code. The next tag, `<%@extension name="htmlb" prefix="htmlb"%>` is only necessary if you work with HTMLB: This tag is used to link the HTMLB extensions. If you write pure HTML code into the layout, that line isn't needed.

As is the case with HTML, HTMLB contains an opening and a closing tag. The tag `<htmlb:content>` which is on the highest level is closed at the end with `</htmlb:content>`. However, there are also some tags that close themselves as they contain the ending "/>", for instance `<htmlb:tableViewColumn columnName="LAST_NAME"/>`.

```
<%@page language="abap"%>
<%@extension name="htmlb" prefix="htmlb"%>

<htmlb:content design="design2003">
  <htmlb:page title = " ">
    <htmlb:form>

      <htmlb:textView    text     = "Hello World!"
                         design   = "EMPHASIZED" />
```

Listing 4.1 Predefined Layout

1 In the following sections, we'll only be able to briefly mention the capabilities of HTMLB. To learn more about this area, you should refer to the book *BSP Extensions: How to master Web Reporting with HTMLB* (SAP PRESS Essentials 2004).

```
        <htmlb:button        text         = "Press Me"
                             onClick      = "myClickHandler" />


      </htmlb:form>
    </htmlb:page>
  </htmlb:content>
```

Listing 4.1 Predefined Layout

An HTMLB page is always structured as follows:

```
<htmlb:content>
  <htmlb:page>
      ...
  </htmlb:page>
</htmlb:content>
```

or

```
<htmlb:content>
  <htmlb:document>
    <htmlb:documentHead>
        ...
    </htmlb:documentHead>
    <htmlb:documentBody>
        ...
    </htmlb:documentBody>
  </htmlb:document>
</htmlb:content>
```

If, for instance, you want to link files in the header area of the HTML code, you should choose the second structure. If you don't want to touch upon the header area, which is what we are doing in our application, you can choose the first structure.

The representation of our phone list is realized by Listing 4.2. Enter the source code from this listing into the layout of your BSP page and activate the BSP page. In order to avoid having to type the entire code manually you can drag and drop the HTMLB elements to the layout area.[2] To do that, proceed as follows:

1. Click on **Tag Browser** in the Object Navigator.
2. Open **BSP Extensions · Transportable · htmlb**. There you can find the available HTMLB elements (see Figure 4.13).

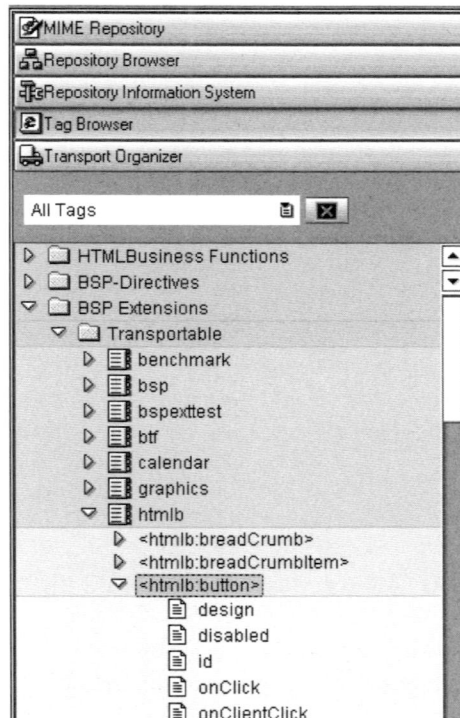

Figure 4.13 Tag Browser

3. Click on the relevant HTMLB element, keep the mouse button pressed and drag the element to the layout area (*drag & drop*).
4. For most of the HTMLB elements, you must add attributes. If you open the individual elements, you can view the possible attributes.
5. By double-clicking on the individual elements, you can navigate to the documentation. In addition to the tag description and examples, the documentation describes all attributes and specifies those that are mandatory.

The source code in Listing 4.2 begins with the header area described above. The next HTMLB element in our

---

2 Alternatively, you can download the source code from the website for this book at *http://www.sap-press.com* and copy it to the relevant position.

application is the `<htmlb:form>` tag. This tag is required if you want to process input data, which means that a form is built.

We'll include the input data and the results list in *trays* (`<htmlb:tray>`). Trays enable you to easily group elements on the screen. At the same time, a user can collapse a tray if necessary, as shown in Figure 4.14. This collapsing can be achieved without any server request, with JavaScript alone, which makes the function very fast.

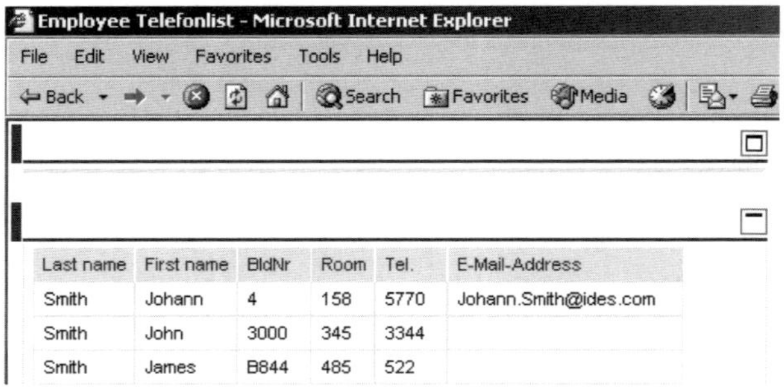

Figure 4.14   Employee List With Collapsed Selection

Trays always have the following structure:

```
<htmlb:tray id="TrayId">
  <htmlb:trayBody>
    ...
  </htmlb:trayBody>
</htmlb:tray>
```

There are two label fields within the selection data, two input fields, and a button. These elements must be grouped according to their relationships to each other. For such groupings, the *GridLayout* (`<htmlb:gridLayout>`) is available. In contrast to the similar HTML tag `<table>` the size of the GridLayout is defined via the parameters `columnIndex` and `rowIndex`. This enables you to address individual cells by using the tag `<GridLayoutCell>`.

We'll use *TextViews* (`<htmlb:textView>`) for labeling the input fields. That way, we can be sure that the text is output in the appropriate size and font.

```
<%@page language="abap"%>
<%@extension name="htmlb" prefix="htmlb"%>

<htmlb:content design="design2003">
  <htmlb:page title = "Employee phone list ">
    <htmlb:form>
      <%-- Input selection data --%>
      <htmlb:tray id="selection"
                  width="450">
        <htmlb:trayBody>
          <htmlb:gridLayout columnSize="3"
                            rowSize="2"
                            width="300">

            <%-- Label Last Name --%>
            <htmlb:gridLayoutCell columnIndex="1" rowIndex="1">
              <htmlb:textView>Last Name</htmlb:textView>
            </htmlb:gridLayoutCell>

            <%-- Input Last Name --%>
            <htmlb:gridLayoutCell columnIndex="2" rowIndex="1">
              <htmlb:inputField id="lastname"
                                value="<%=lastname%>"/>
```

Listing 4.2   Layout of the Phone List

```
    </htmlb:gridLayoutCell>

    <%-- Label First Name --%>
    <htmlb:gridLayoutCell columnIndex="1" rowIndex="2">
      <htmlb:textView>First Name</htmlb:textView>
    </htmlb:gridLayoutCell>

    <%-- Input First Name --%>
    <htmlb:gridLayoutCell columnIndex="2" rowIndex="2">
      <htmlb:inputField id="fstname"
                        value="<%=fstname%>"/>
    </htmlb:gridLayoutCell>

    <%-- Search Button --%>
    <htmlb:gridLayoutCell columnIndex="3"
                          rowIndex="2"
                          horizontalAlignment="left" >
      <htmlb:button id="search"
                    text="Search"
                    onClick="ButtonClick"/>
    </htmlb:gridLayoutCell>
  </htmlb:gridLayout>

  </htmlb:trayBody>
</htmlb:tray>
<br>
<%-- Output Employee List --%>
<htmlb:tray id="emplist"
            width="450">
  <htmlb:trayBody>
    <htmlb:tableView id="tvemplist"
                     table="<%=COMMLIST_T%>">
      <htmlb:tableViewColumns>
        <htmlb:tableViewColumn columnName="LAST_NAME"/>
        <htmlb:tableViewColumn columnName="FIRSTNAME"/>
        <htmlb:tableViewColumn columnName="BLDING_NO"/>
        <htmlb:tableViewColumn columnName="ROOM_NO"/>
        <htmlb:tableViewColumn columnName="PHONENO1"/>
        <htmlb:tableViewColumn columnName="USRID_LONG"/>
      </htmlb:tableViewColumns>
    </htmlb:tableView>

  </htmlb:trayBody>
```

Listing 4.2 Layout of the Phone List (cont.)

```
        </htmlb:tray>

      </htmlb:form>
    </htmlb:page>
  </htmlb:content>
```

Listing 4.2 Layout of the Phone List (cont.)

The input fields are created using the tag element `<htmlb:inputField>`. You should make sure that the `id` and the variable have the same name. In the page attributes of our BSP page, we marked the selection variables with the **auto** indicator, which means that the variables can be automatically filled via URL parameters or form fields. The input field `id` is implemented in the HTML form field so that we no longer need read out the input values. To keep the input value, we add the "variable value" to `<htmlb:inputField>`: The page directive `<%=...%>` can be used to read ABAP variables.

The tag element `<htmlb:button>` is used to implement the **Search** button. The `id` attribute can later be queried in the events, which is particularly necessary if the user interface contains more than one button. The `text` attribute defines the labeling of the button. The `onClick` attribute is passed as an event to the event handler and can be used for the continued execution of the program. If neither `onClick` nor `onClientClick` is set, the button is displayed as disabled and can't be used.

The results list is displayed in a TableView (`<htmlb:tableView>`) which is one of the most powerful HTMLB elements. TableViews enable you to easily output internal tables and you can define which columns you want to output in which order. All functions of a good table display, such as scrolling, sorting or re-sorting are automatically provided. The structure of a TableView can vary. In our application we'll use the following structure:

```
<htmlb:tableView id="TableViewID"
               table="<%=<Table>%>">
  <htmlb:tableViewColumns>
    <htmlb:tableViewColumn
        columnName="<Column_1>"/>
    ...
    <htmlb:tableViewColumn
        columnName="<Column_n>"/>
```

```
  </htmlb:tableViewColumns>
</htmlb:tableView>
```

First, we transfer the table in the `<htmlb:tableView>` tag, and then we define which columns are to be displayed in which order.

Data Retrieval

As we want to separate the business logic from the presentation logic, we don't want to perform the data retrieval process in the events, but in the relevant application class. So let's develop that data-retrieval method.

1. Start the Class Builder (Transaction SE24) via SAP GUI.

2. Enter the name of our application class ("Z_CL_BSP_ EMP_COMM") into the **Object Type** field and click on **Change**.

3. Now we create the new method, `GET_EMP_ COMMLIST`. This method is an **Instance Method** which can be seen and called from external systems (**Public**). As a description you can enter, "Retrieves communication data of employees" (see Figure 4.15).

4. Click on **Parameters**. We'll now define the import and export parameters of the method. Set the first and last names as import parameters (**Importing**), and the employee list as export parameter (**Exporting**). Figure 4.16 shows the exact details.

5. Click on the **Methods** button to return to the methods overview and save your work.

6. Now we can begin the implementation of the method. You can access the code of the method by double-clicking on the method name **GET_EMP_ COMMLIST**. Then implement the code shown in Listing 4.3.

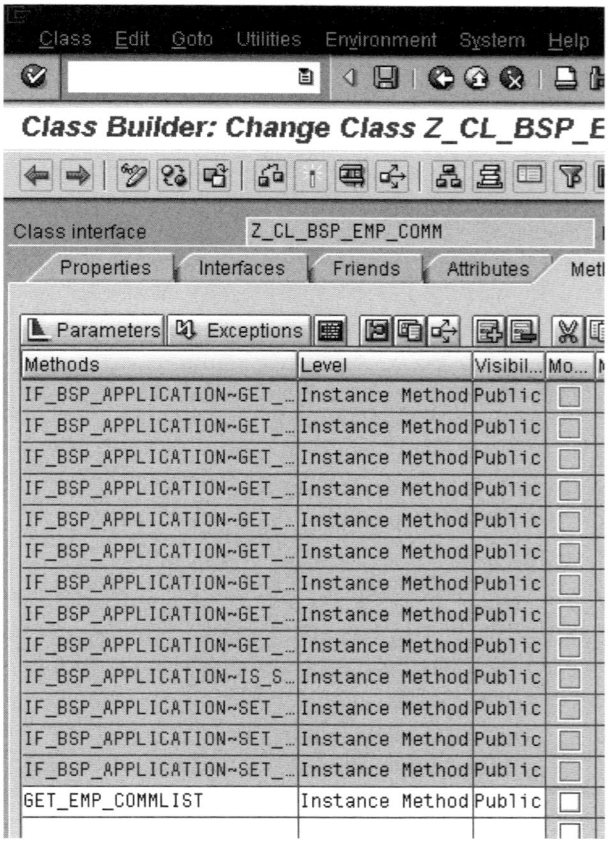

Figure 4.15 New Method GET_EMP_COMMLIST

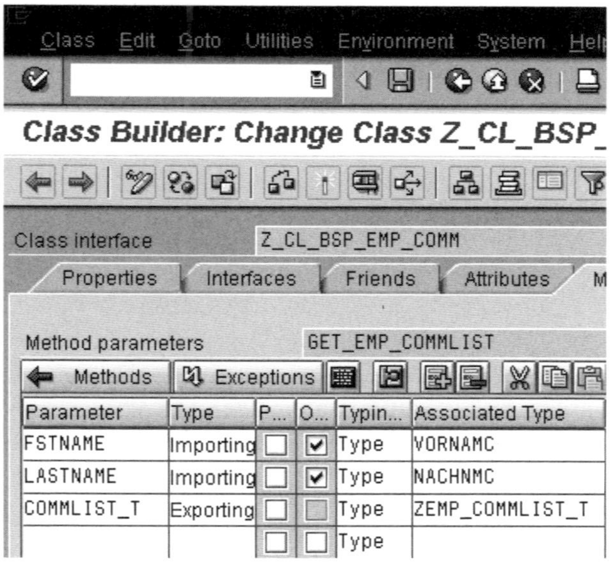

Figure 4.16 Parameters for the GET_EMP_COMMLIST Method

```
METHOD get_emp_commlist .
* Data definition
  DATA: i_rfcdest TYPE rfcdest.
  DATA: wa_commlist          LIKE LINE OF commlist_t.
  DATA:
        itab_org_assignment   TYPE TABLE OF bapip0001b,
        wa_org_assignment     LIKE LINE  OF itab_org_assignment,
        itab_personal_data    TYPE TABLE OF bapip0002b,
        wa_personal_data      LIKE LINE  OF itab_personal_data,
        itab_internal_control TYPE TABLE OF bapip0032b,
        wa_internal_control   LIKE LINE  OF itab_internal_control,
        itab_communication    TYPE TABLE OF bapip0105b,
        wa_communication      LIKE LINE  OF itab_communication.

* Initialization
* Read RFC Destination - it is useful to move this
* to a separate method
```

Listing 4.3 GET_EMP_COMMLIST Method

```
  SELECT SINGLE rfcdest FROM zbsp_rfcdest INTO i_rfcdest
                  WHERE sysname = 'R3HR'.
* If no RFC Dest. Is maintained, the BAPI is called on a
* separate system
  IF sy-subrc <> 0.
    i_rfcdest = 'NONE'.
  ENDIF.


* Call BAPI
  CALL FUNCTION 'BAPI_EMPLOYEE_GETDATA'
    DESTINATION i_rfcdest
    EXPORTING
      lastname_m       = lastname
      fstname_m        = fstname
      authority_check  = 'X'
    TABLES
      org_assignment   = itab_org_assignment
      personal_data    = itab_personal_data
      internal_control = itab_internal_control
      communication    = itab_communication.


* In the next step we assume that Personal_Data is
* the main table
  LOOP AT itab_personal_data INTO wa_personal_data.
*  Read organizational data
    READ TABLE itab_org_assignment
       WITH KEY perno = wa_personal_data-perno
       INTO wa_org_assignment.
    IF sy-subrc <> 0.
      CLEAR wa_org_assignment.
    ENDIF.
* Read personal data
    READ TABLE itab_internal_control
       WITH KEY perno = wa_personal_data-perno
       INTO wa_internal_control.
    IF sy-subrc <> 0.
      CLEAR wa_internal_control.
    ENDIF.
* Read communication data
    READ TABLE itab_communication
       WITH KEY perno = wa_personal_data-perno
                subtype = '0010'
       INTO wa_communication.
```

Listing 4.3 GET_EMP_COMMLIST Method (cont.)

```
  IF sy-subrc <> 0.
    CLEAR wa_communication.
  ENDIF.

* Fill own data structure
  MOVE-CORRESPONDING wa_personal_data TO wa_commlist.
  MOVE-CORRESPONDING wa_org_assignment TO wa_commlist.
  MOVE-CORRESPONDING wa_internal_control TO wa_commlist.
  MOVE-CORRESPONDING wa_communication TO wa_commlist.

  APPEND wa_commlist TO commlist_t.
  ENDLOOP.

ENDMETHOD.
```

Listing 4.3   GET_EMP_COMMLIST Method (cont.)

The GET_EMP_COMMLIST Method

In the next step, we want to call the method just developed from our BSP application. There are several options available for doing that.

Before we go into detail, it will help to reiterate the call times for the different events. Figure 4.17 illustrates the control flow of a BSP.

► First, the OnCreate event is run through, provided the application is stateless. If the application is stateful, the OnCreate event is processed only at the first call.

► Then follows the OnRequest event, which is used for restoring the internal data structures from the request. This event is predominantly needed for stateless applications.

► If the request results from an input page, it can happen that the OnInputProcessing event handler is called. If that's not the case, the application directly navigates to the OnInitialization event. This event is responsible for data retrieval.

► In the next step, the stored layout is called. Here the actual page construction takes place.

► Finally, the calculated layout can be overwritten by calling OnManipulation. The newly calculated result is then sent to the browser.

Readers from the R/3 world are probably inclined to place the data-retrieval process in the OnInputProcessing event. Basically, that's not wrong at all, given that a user's input is responded to in that event. However, we want to work with a stateless application, and therefore we must temporarily store the data and read it from the cache when the page is called again.

Thus, as an alternative we can transfer the input values of the selection to the application and perform the data retrieval in the OnInitialization event. This procedure provides the enormous advantage of making our application reusable. If for instance we transfer the selection parameters via URL parameters, any application can fill these parameters and call the application. Now we'll proceed with the implementation in the OnInitialization event.

1. In SAP GUI, go to the Object Navigator and open our BSP application, **Z_EMP_COMM**.

2. Open the detail view of the *default.htm* page.

3. Go to the **OnInitialization** event handler.

4. Implement the call for the GET_EMP_COMMLIST method, as shown in Figure 4.18.

5. Save and activate the BSP page.

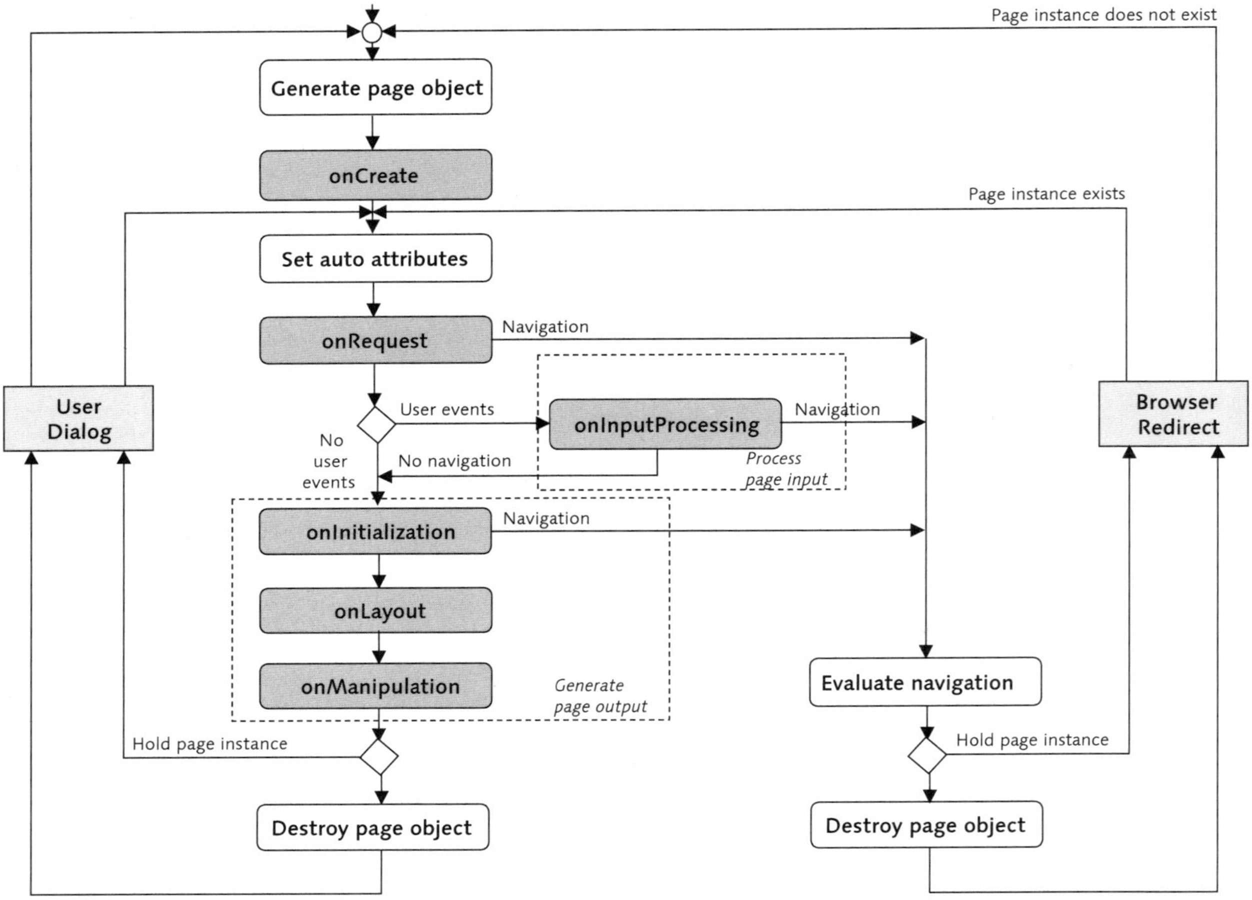

Figure 4.17 Control Flow for a Business Server Page

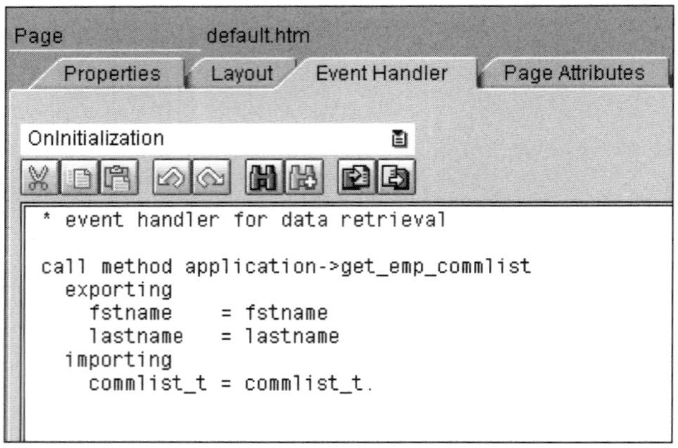

Figure 4.18 Code in the Event Handler "OnInitialization"

```
* event handler for data retrieval

call method application->get_emp_commlist
  exporting
    fstname    = fstname
    lastname   = lastname
  importing
    commlist_t = commlist_t.
```

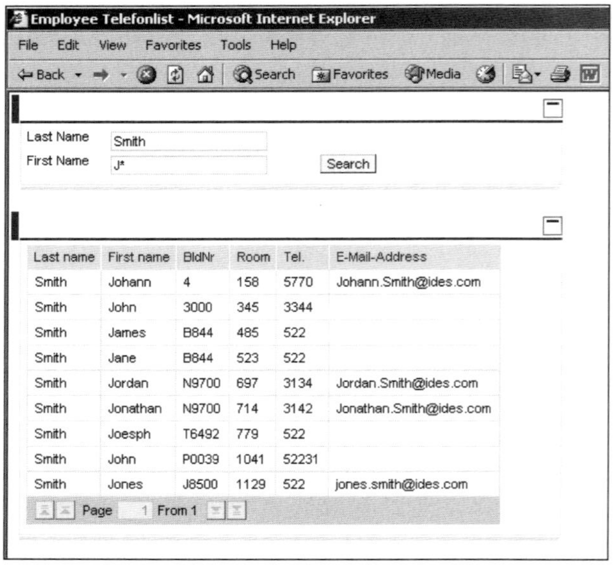

Figure 4.19 Testing "Employee List"

Now that the application is complete, you can test the page: Open the context menu of *default.htm* and select **Test**. In the example shown here the data of the IDES system is displayed (see Figure 4.19).

4.3 Authentication

During testing, you were prompted to enter a user name and password. There are several ways to disable an authentication in order to make the application accessible for every portal user. You can either solve this issue in the portal or directly in SAP Web Application Server.

In our example, we'll connect a generic user with the application. This means that the application always runs with the predefined user, both inside and outside of the portal.

1. Go to the maintenance of the HTTP service tree (Transaction SICF).
2. Open the node **default_host · sap · bc · bsp · sap**.
3. The system displays all BSP applications. At this point you can activate and deactivate applications so that they can't be called from an external system. Open the **z_emp_comm** node by double-clicking on it.
4. Click on the **pencil icon** to change into the editing mode.
5. Maintain the **Client**, the **User,** and the **Password** (see Figure 4.20). Create a separate user: a system user rather than a dialog user.

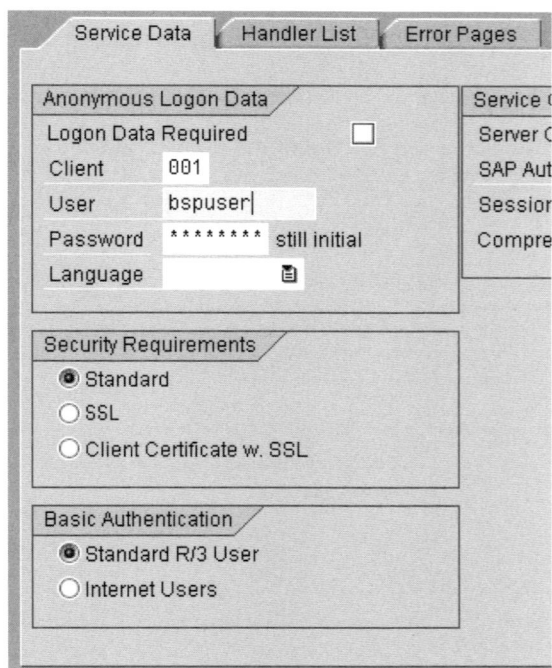

Figure 4.20 Maintaining a Default User for BSP

4.4 Portal Integration

Having completed all preparatory tasks, we can now connect our application with the portal from which it can then be called. For this purpose, we'll use the folder structure we created in Chapter 2.

However, before you can create an iView—that's the technology used to integrate external applications into SAP Enterprise Portal—we must first make the system on which the Business Server Page runs known to the portal.

1. Logon to SAP Enterprise Portal 6.0.
2. Navigate to **System Administration · System Configuration · System Landscape**.
3. Open the node **Portal Content · MyContent** under the **Browse** tab.
4. Create a subfolder called **Systems** in the *MyContent* folder.
5. Open the context menu of **MyContent** and select **New · Folder**. The folder name and folder ID are "Systems", and the original language is **English**. Click on **Finish**.
6. Select **Close wizard** in the dialog that opens and click **OK**.

In the following steps we'll create a new system.

1. Open the context menu of **Systems,** and select **New · System**.
2. Select **R/3 system with Load Balancing** from the list of templates and click on the **Next** button.
3. You can choose any **System Name** and **System ID**, but they should resemble the actual system name; in our case the system name is "APP01". Select the original language **English,** and click on **Next**.
4. Verify your entries, and confirm them by clicking on **Finish**.
5. Then select **Open object for editing** because the system can't be used yet in its current state.
6. In the next step we'll create a system alias. To do that, select the **System Aliases** entry from the dropdown box in the upper right-hand area.
7. Enter an alias, for instance APP01, and click on the **Add** button. This completes the creation of a system alias.

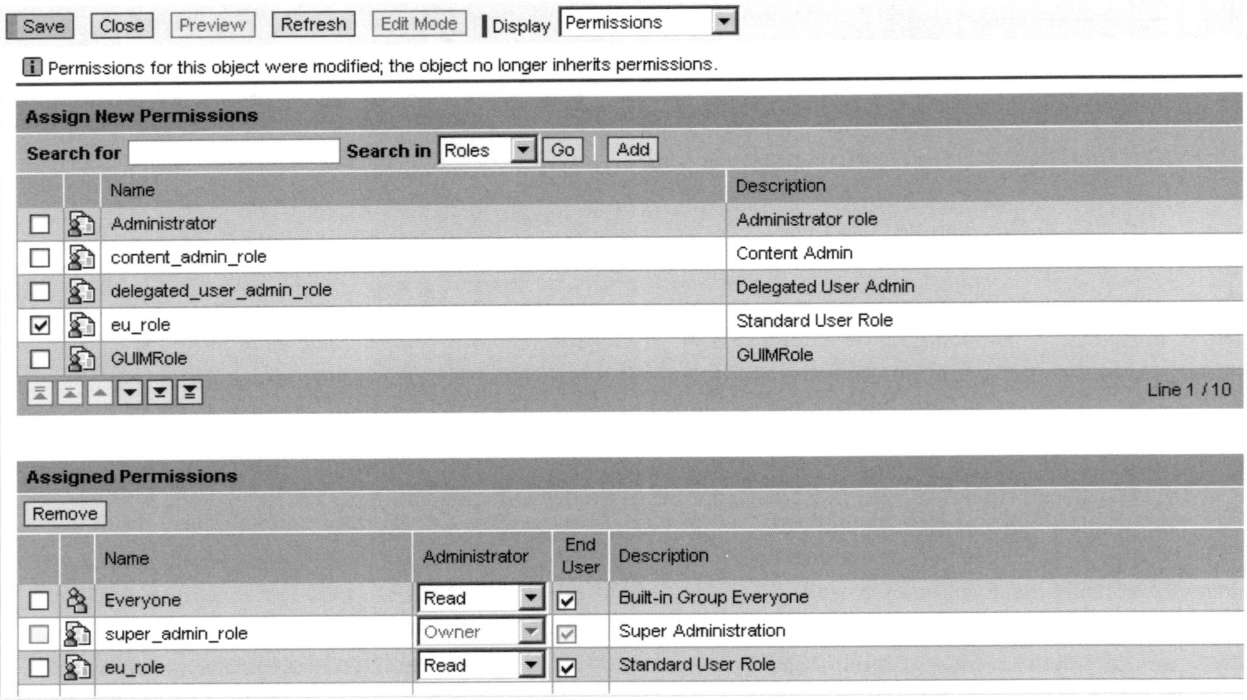

Figure 4.21 Authorization Editor for Systems

8. Now we must store the connection information for SAP Web Application Server. Select the **Object** entry from the dropdown box in the upper right-hand area. Select **Web Application Server (WAS)** as the property category.

9. In the **Host Name** field, enter the host name of your SAP Web AS including the port number, for example "app01.myserver.com:8000".

10. The **WAS protocol** is **http**. Save your entries by clicking on the **Save** button.

The new system is not visible for every portal user, which is why we still have to define the system authorizations. To do that, select the **Authorizations** entry from the dropdown box in the upper right-hand area.

To make the application available to every user you must also grant a full system access to every user. The **eu_role** role is the default role every user should have. Hence we'll use that role.

1. Find the role **eu_role**, highlight it and add it to the list of assigned authorizations, as shown in Figure 4.21.

2. Check the **User** box, and save the change by clicking on the **Save** button.

3. We now want to test the connection to the new system. Select **Connection Tests** from the upper right-hand area.

4. Highlight the entry **SAP Web AS Connection** and click on **Test**. If the test was successful, a message is displayed similar to the one shown in Figure 4.22.

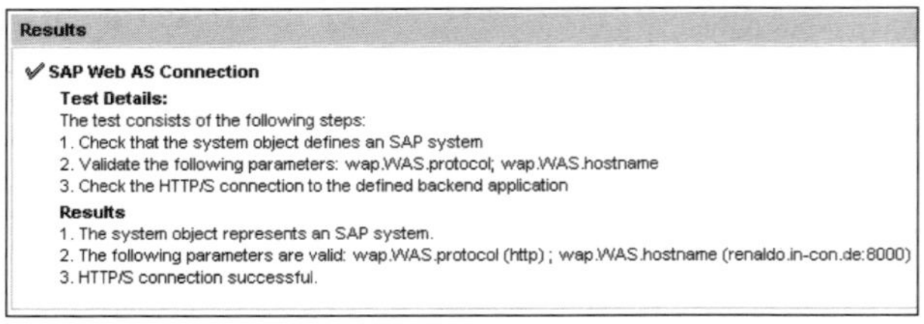

Figure 4.22 Successful Connection Test

Creating the iView

Now that we have successfully created and tested the system, we can create the iView. iViews are used to integrate applications into the portal.

1. Select **Content Administration · Portal Content** and open **Portal Content · MyContent · iViews**.

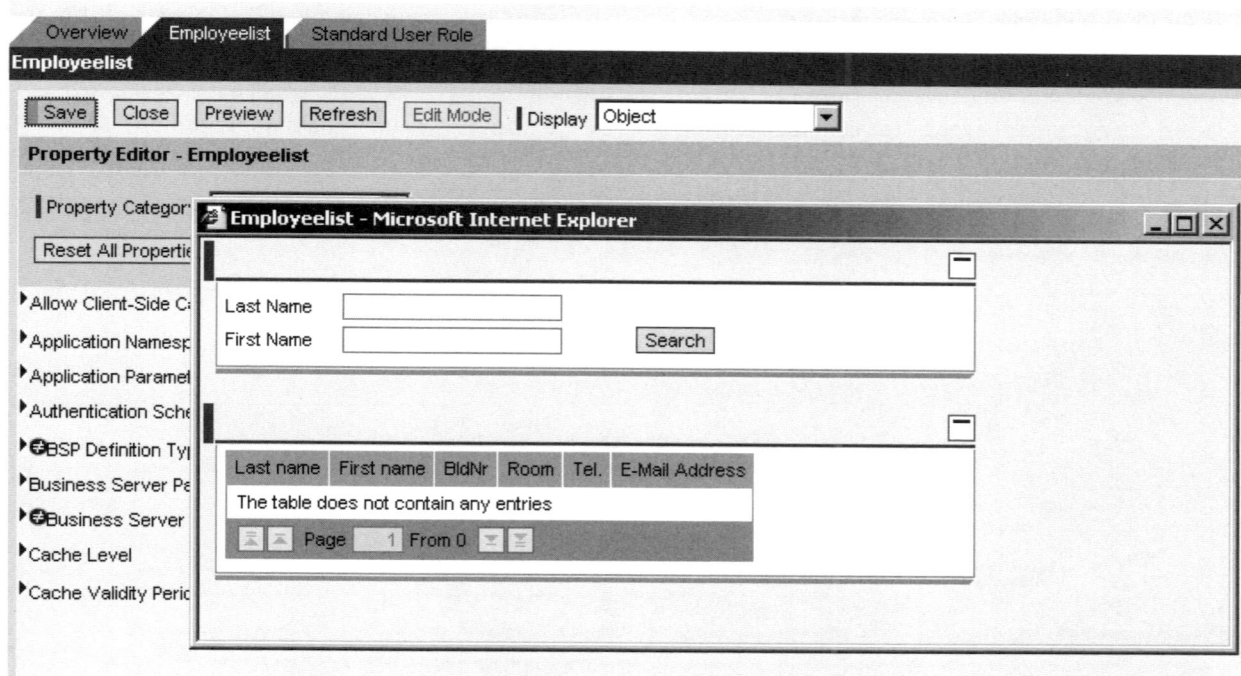

Figure 4.23 iView Preview

2. Create a subfolder called "Employee list" in the *iViews* folder.

3. Now you can create the iView. Open the context menu of the **Employee list** folder and select **New · iView**.

4. Select **iView SAP BSP** from the list of templates displayed and click on the **Next** button.

5. Enter "Employee list" in the **iView Name** and **iView ID** fields, and the original language is again **English**. Click on **Next**.

6. Then you can select the application variant. As we aren't using an alias, you can accept the pre-selected entry **BSP** and click on **Next**.

7. Now we have to take care of the application parameters: Select the newly created connection to your SAP Web Application Server from the list of systems. You can accept the values in the fields **Customer Namespace** and **Application Namespace**. Enter the name of our BSP application ("Z_EMP_COMM") in the Business Server Page Application field. The **Home Page** is "default.htm". Confirm this by clicking **Next**.

8. You can check your entries in the summary. Check the **Open for editing when wizard completes** checkbox and click on **Finish**.

You can already test the portal integration by clicking on the **Preview** button. As you can see in Figure 4.23, the user interface of the BSP layout automatically adjusts itself to the portal environment.

Assigning the iView to the Role

Now we want to make our application available to every user. To do that, we'll use the role **eu_user** which is the default role for every user.

When creating new users, you should make sure that at least this role is always assigned.

1. Logon to the portal as a content administrator and navigate to **Content Administration · Portal Content**.

2. Open **Portal Content · Portal Users · Standard Portal Users**.

3. Open the Standard User role via the context menu and then select **Open · Object**.

4. Highlight the **Home** node at the top level.
5. Open **Portal Content · MyContent · iViews · Employee List**.
6. In the context menu of the iView Employee List, select **Add iView to Role · Data Link**, as shown in Figure 4.24.

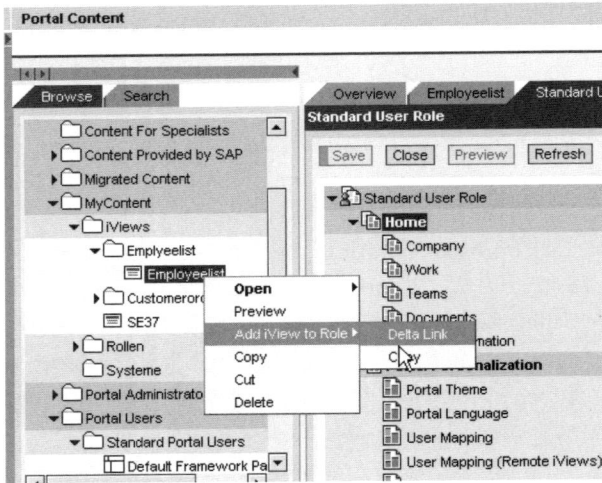

Figure 4.24 Adding the iView to the Role

The iView `Employee list` has thus been added to the default role. Each user assigned to that role can now use our application (see Figure 4.25).

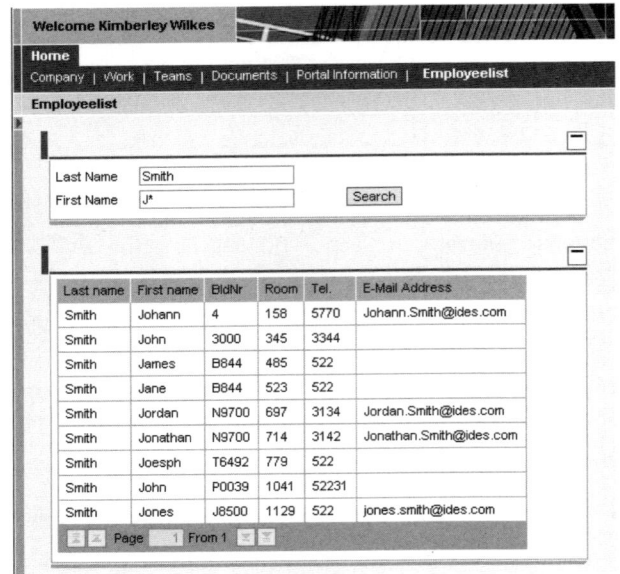

Figure 4.25 Employee List in the Portal

5 Tips and Tricks

This chapter provides tips and tricks to make your life easier as a developer. Section 5.1 describes the SAP Enterprise Portal Sneak Preview from the SAP Developer Network. It focuses specifically on the configurations needed for creating the applications developed in this book. Section 5.2 provides several troubleshooting options. You'll learn where you can find trace and log files in the Java environment, how to debug, and how you can delete your application.

5.1 Sneak Preview

An excellent way to familiarize yourself with SAP Enterprise Portal 6.0 and the development environment is provided by the *Sneak Preview*. You can download the current version via the *SAP Developer Network* (SDN). Just register free of charge at *http://sdn.sap.com*, and then go to the **Downloads** area. By the way: The SDN forums and weblogs are excellent sources of information, not only for SAP Enterprise Portal.

If you want to reconstruct the programming examples described in this book using the Sneak Preview, some additional configurations are necessary.

Configuring the SLD

In the System Landscape Directory (SLD), you configure the connections to other systems. Before you can set up the R/3 systems you want to use you must configure the SLD.

1. Start the SAP J2EE engine.
2. Use the web browser to call the following URL: *http://<yourPortalserver>:<Portnumber>/sld*.

3. You will be prompted to authenticate yourself. The user name is "Administrator", and the password is the one you specified during the portal installation. If you run Support Package 11, it is "admin".
4. Click on **Administration**, then on **Server-Settings**. Enter the host name of your machine into the **Object Server** field and click on **Set**. Click on **Administration** again and start the server. To do that, click on **Start Server**. The status indicator next to the button should now change from *Stopped* to *Running*.
5. Once the SLD server has started up correctly, you must import the CIM models. To do that, click on **Import** in the **Administration** area. Select the files to be imported and click on **Import**.
6. In a Sneak Preview installation you can find the CIM files to be imported in the following directory: *C:\usr\sap\<System ID>\SYS\global\sld\model*. Import the files *cimsap.zip* and *CR_Content.zip*.

Connecting the SLD and SAP J2EE Engine

Once the SLD is up and running, you must connect it with the SAP J2EE engine.

1. Start the J2EE engine if it isn't running yet.
2. Start Visual Administrator (*C:\usr\sap\J2E\<System ID>\JC00\j2ee\admin\go.bat*).
3. Select **Connect** and log on to the J2EE engine. To be able to do that you need a user ID with administrator rights.

Logon Problems (Visual Administrator)
At this point you may encounter some problems. Typically, when you start Visual Administrator the system automatically suggests a connection. If it doesn't, you can create a new one.
The **User Name** is "Administrator" or "admin", the password is either the one you specified during installation or "admin". The **Host name** is your own host, the **HTTP port** is 8100+instance, most probably it's 8101. For further information, please refer to SAP Note 730400.

4. After logging on, select the **Cluster** tab, expand the **Server, Services** node, and select **SLD Data Supplier**.
5. Select **CIM Client Generation Settings,** and specify the required http connection parameters to establish a connection to the SLD, as shown in Figure 5.1.
6. Save the data by clicking on the **Save** button.
7. Click on **CIM Client Test** to test the connection to the CIM client.
8. If the test is successful, you can close the J2EE Engine Administrator Console. If not, you must correct the connection parameters.

You have now defined the connection to the running SLD which can now be used by your applications.

Maintaining SAP Systems in the SLD
If you want to perform an RFC call of a pure R/3 system from a Web Dynpro application, the Java environment requires the connection information for the model declaration and the subsequent RFC. For this reason, the required R/3 system must be maintained in the SLD.
1. Call the following URL in the web browser: *http://<yourPortalserver>:<Portnumber>/sld*.
2. Select the menu item **Technical Landscape**.
3. Select **Web AS ABAP** in the **Technical System Type** field and click on **New Technical System...**
4. Select **Web AS ABAP** in the **Technical System Type** window and click on **Next**.
5. Maintain the system ID (**SID**) and additional access data in the **System Details,** and click on **Next**.
6. Maintain the data for accessing the message server in the **Message Server and Central Application Server** window, and click on **Next**.
7. The wizard then brings you to the **Additional Application Server (optional)** window. Enter a **Hostname** and **Instance Number,** and click on **Add**. Then click on the **Next** button to navigate to the next window.
8. In the next window, you must maintain at least the access to a client and then click on **Next**.
9. Then specify the **Software Products And Components** of your R/3 system. If for instance you select the entry **SAP R/3 Enterprise 47X110**, the system

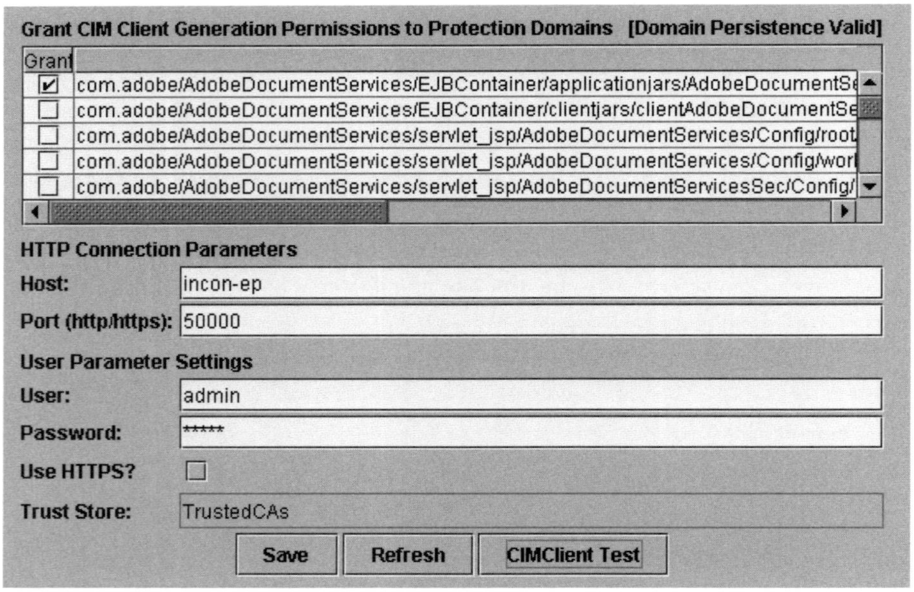

Figure 5.1 CIM Client Generation Settings

displays the components as shown in Figure 5.2. If necessary, you might have to deselect some of the components before you click on **Finish**.

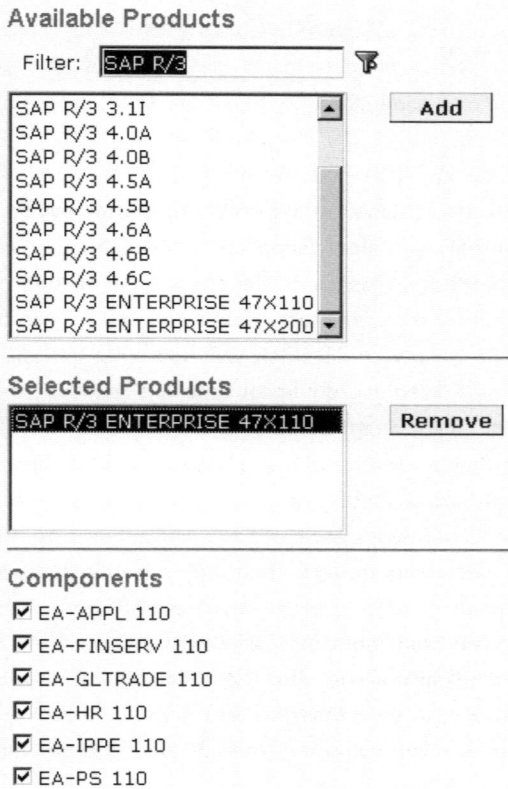

Available Products

Filter: [SAP R/3]

```
SAP R/3 3.1I                          Add
SAP R/3 4.0A
SAP R/3 4.0B
SAP R/3 4.5A
SAP R/3 4.5B
SAP R/3 4.6A
SAP R/3 4.6B
SAP R/3 4.6C
SAP R/3 ENTERPRISE 47X110
SAP R/3 ENTERPRISE 47X200
```

Selected Products

```
SAP R/3 ENTERPRISE 47X110             Remove
```

Components

☑ EA-APPL 110

☑ EA-FINSERV 110

☑ EA-GLTRADE 110

☑ EA-HR 110

☑ EA-IPPE 110

☑ EA-PS 110

Figure 5.2 Assigning Installed Products

5.2 Troubleshooting During Web Dynpro Development

Even a development expert sometimes faces a situation in which a program doesn't run as it should, or doesn't run at all. We want to introduce some possible solutions.

Where Can I Find Trace or Log Files?

If you call a BAPI from a Web Dynpro application via an RFC, there can be many reasons as to why this call fails. Perhaps the system you called is currently not available, the RFC module interface has changed and must be re-generated and so forth. The RFC module call is encapsulated via the `try` command, and in case of an error a trace is written, as shown in Listing 5.1.

This trace is located on the J2EE server in the following directory: *C:\usr\sap\<System ID>\j2ee\cluster\server0\log*. There you can find a file with the extension *.trc* (e.g. *defaultTrace.0.trc*).

How Can I Switch On the Debugging Mode?

Debugging is one of the most important and powerful tools of a developer. To debug a Web Dynpro application, the server must be set to the debugging mode. For this reason, you must check the J2EE server settings in SAP NetWeaver Developer Studio:

1. In SAP NetWeaver Developer Studio, select **Window · Preferences**.
2. Select the **SAP J2EE Engine** node in the **Preferences** window.
3. Depending on whether the J2EE engine runs on a local system or on an external one, you must select the corresponding option. If the J2EE engine runs locally, you can use the **Browse...** button to make your selection. If you work remotely, maintain the **Message Server Host** and the **Message Server Port** (see Figure 5.3).

When you have verified that a connection exists between SAP NetWeaver Developer Studio and the J2EE engine, you can switch on the **Debugging Mode**. A precondition

```
try{
  // Call function module BAPI_SALESORDER_GETLIST
  wdContext.currentBAPI_SALESORDER_GETLIST_INPUTElement().modelObject().execute();
  }
catch (Exception ex)
  {
  // If an error occurs, output stack
  ex.printStackTrace();
  }
```

Listing 5.1 Writing a Trace

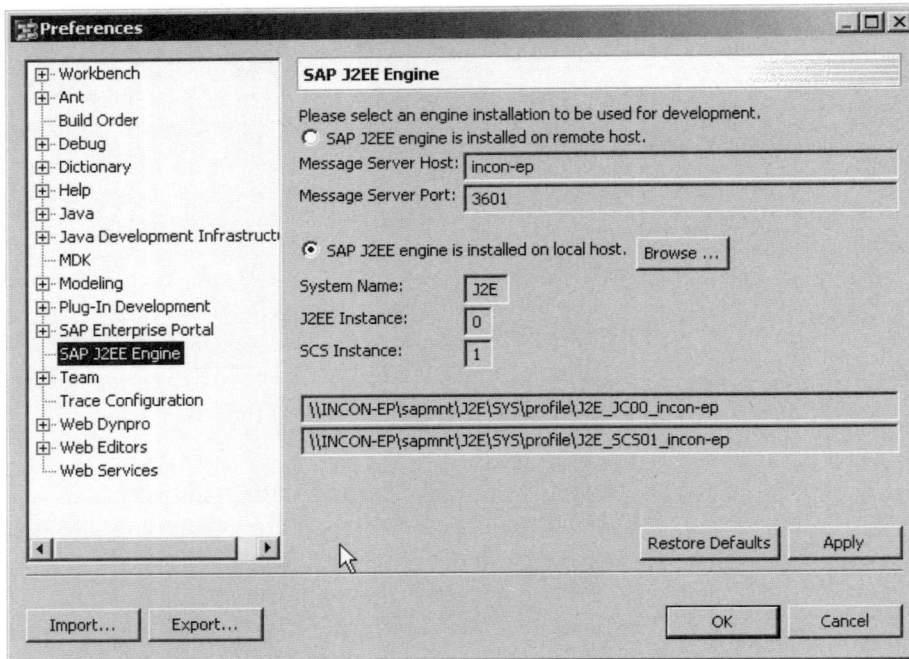

Figure 5.3   J2EE Server Settings in SAP NetWeaver Developer Studio

for this is that **Productive Use** is set to **NO**. If it is set to **YES**, you must perform the following steps:

1. Open the J2EE Engine view by selecting **Window · Show View · Other...** and then **J2EE · J2EE Engine**.
2. Open the node **Remote engine · <hostname>: <3601> · J2E instance 00 on <hostname> · server0**, as shown in Figure 5.4.
3. Open the context menu of **server0** and activate debugging by selecting **Enable debugging of process**.
4. Then the J2EE restarts automatically.

Another option for enabling the debugging mode is to use the **Configtool**. Make sure the system is not a production system, and proceed as follows:

1. Start the Configtool via *C:\usr\sap\<System ID>\j2ee\ configtool\configtool.bat*.
2. Open the **instance** node. There you'll find a node called **server** with the cluster ID from the J2EE Engine view.
3. Click on the **Debug** tab and select **Debuggable** as well as **Enabled debug mode** (see Figure 5.5).
4. Save your entries and restart the J2EE engine.

How Can I Set Breakpoints?
Now that we enabled debugging for the J2EE engine, we can set breakpoints.

1. Open the point in the implementation at which you want to disrupt the execution.
2. Open the context menu on the frame to the left of the source code and select **Add Breakpoint** (see Figure 5.6).

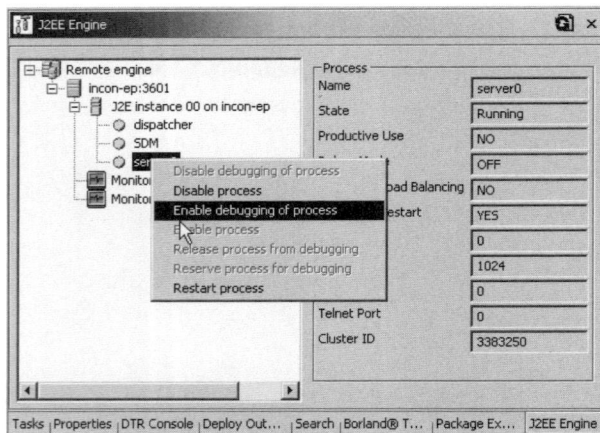

Figure 5.4   Enabling the Debugging Mode

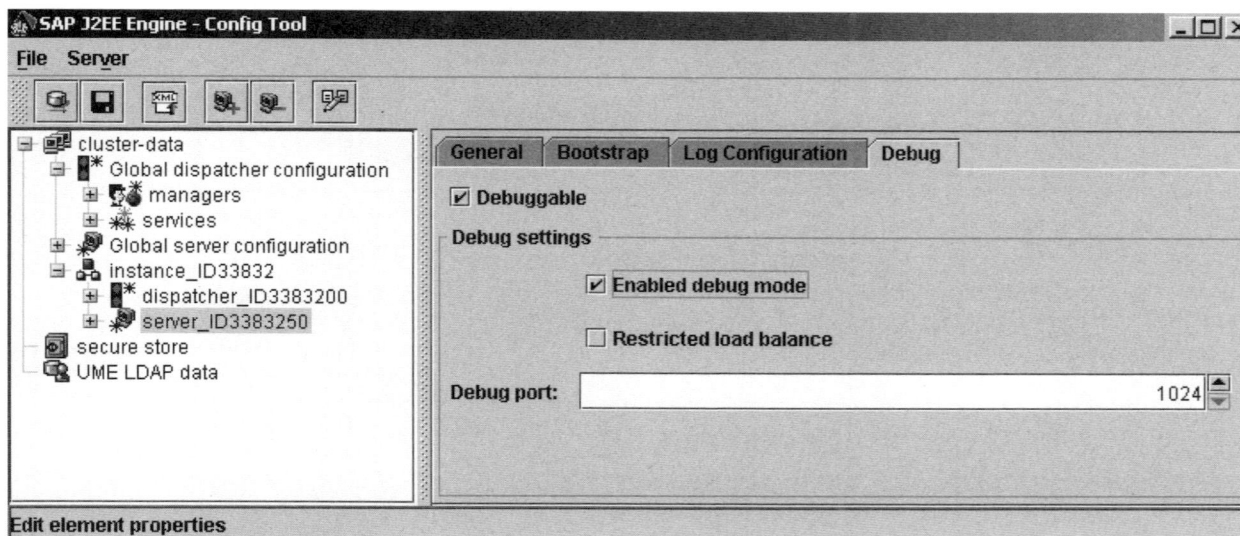

Figure 5.5 Setting the Debug Mode via Configtool

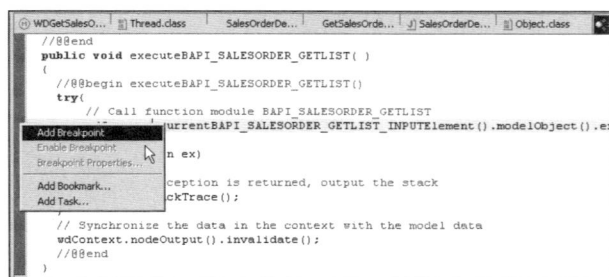

Figure 5.6 Setting a Breakpoint

Once we have set the breakpoint we can start our debugging session.

1. Select **Run · Debug...** from the SAP NetWeaver Developer Studio menu.
2. Select **Web Dynpro-Application** from the list of possible configurations and click on **New**.
3. Use the **Browse...** button to select a project and a Web Dynpro application. Make sure the **Create and deploy archive** checkbox is checked.
4. If no valid J2EE engine has been stored, click on the **J2EE Engine** tab and select a valid instance.
5. Start the debugger by clicking on the **Debug** button.
6. If the program reaches the breakpoint, its execution is interrupted and the debugging mode opens in SAP NetWeaver Developer Studio (see Figure 5.7).

How Can I Delete a Web Dynpro Application on the J2EE Server?

Sometimes it's necessary to delete a Web Dynpro application from the J2EE engine. You may want to permanently delete an application, for example, or you want to delete it because of deployment problems and then redeploy it. In such cases, you should proceed as follows:

1. Start the Software Deployment Manager (SDM) Remote GUI via the following path: *C:\usr\sap\<System ID>\JC00\SDM\program\RemoteGui.bat*.
2. Click on **Connect to SDM Server** and log on. If you are using the Sneak Preview, the password is "sdm".
3. Click on the **Undeployment** tab.
4. Select the relevant application in the left-hand pane and use the arrow key to move it to the right-hand pane (**SDAs selected for Undeployment**).
5. Click on the **Start Undeployment** button (see Figure 5.8).
6. When the undeployment is finished, restart the J2EE engine.

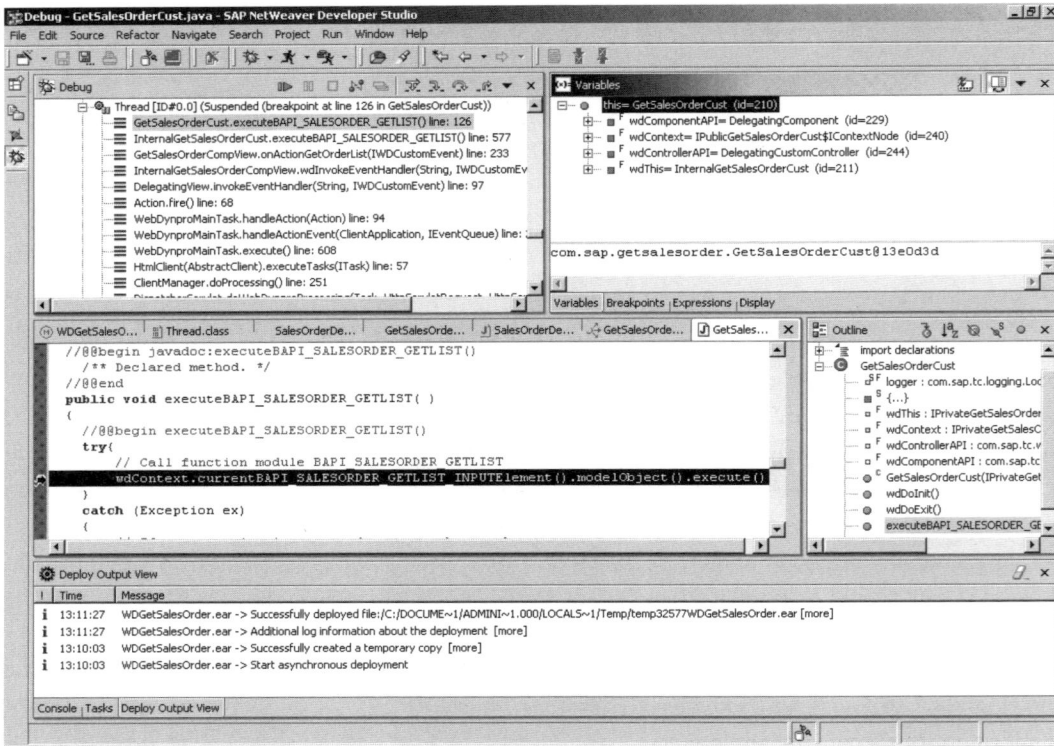

Figure 5.7   Debugging Mode

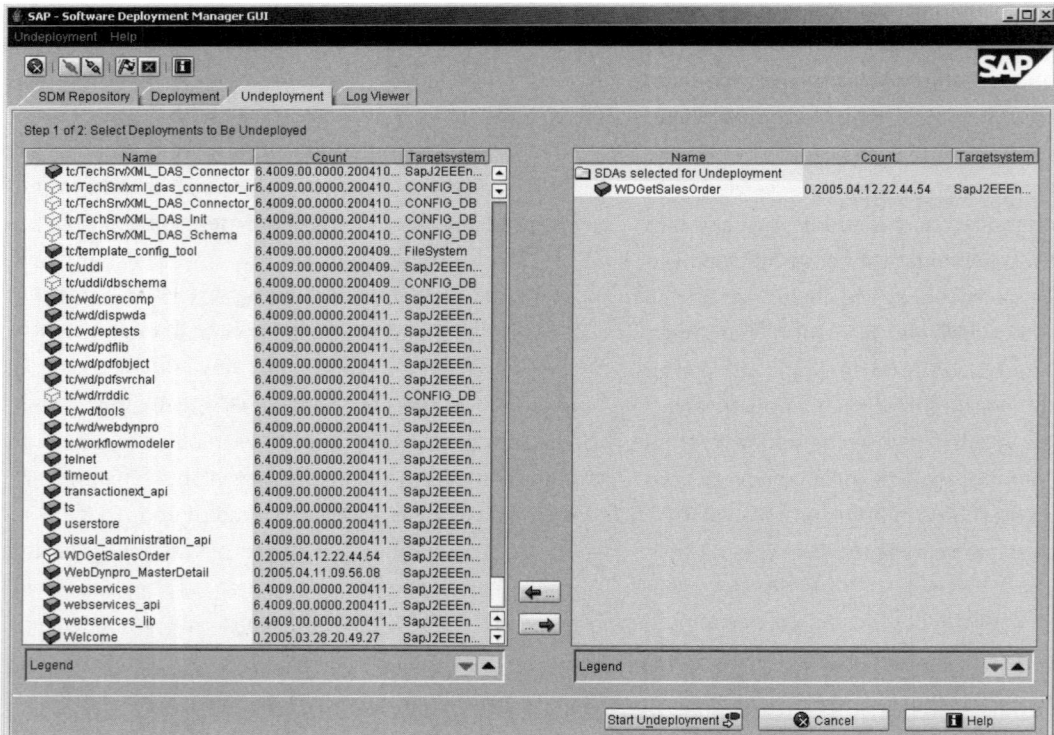

Figure 5.8   Software Deployment Manager (SDM)

6 Summary

Our little expedition through the SAP Enterprise Portal application development world is coming to an end. We have developed a Web Dynpro application, have extensively explored the subject of role-based behavior, and have integrated the application into the portal. We also developed a BSP application for which we made a brief excursion into the HTMLB area. We attended to data acquisition and wrappers, thereby placing our applications in the contexts of employee, customer, and partner portals.

Most of you probably want to know what direction the development environments introduced here are going to move in the future. You're now asking: "Which programming technique should I opt for in order to develop future-proof applications?"

In the Business Server Pages area, the development environment is more or less complete. There will of course be the odd improvement here and enhancement there, especially in the area of BSP extensions. BSPs can be used for developments that can't be realized with Web Dynpro, for instance the creation of an individual layout directly via HTML or the use of JavaScript. This consideration, plus the many applications already developed support the continued existence of BSPs.

However, the future definitely belongs to Web Dynpro developments, the benefits of which have been the subject of this SAP PRESS Essentials book. SAP promotes Web Dynpro as the future user interface, and many applications are already being developed with this technology. Web Dynpro for ABAP soon will be delivered to ramp-up customers. The existing presentations and information available on Web Dynpro for ABAP leave no doubt about the fact that it is more than just an imaginative extension of the development environment.

With Web Dynpro for ABAP, you'll be able to choose whether to make your developments in ABAP or Java. It's nevertheless useful to study the Java environment, because the object structure, contexts, and programming will be similar in both Web Dynpro for ABAP and Web Dynpro for Java.

This perspective and the real-life insight provided by this book should prepare you for future decisions on developing applications in the SAP Enterprise Portal area.

Index

ISBN 978-1-59229-075-8

1st edition 2006, 1st reprint 2007
© 2006 by Galileo Press GmbH
SAP PRESS is an imprint of Galileo Press,
Boston (MA), USA
Bonn, Germany

Copy Editor John Parker, UCG, Inc., Boston, MA
Cover Design Vera Brauner
Printed in Germany